ANCHOR BOOKS

INSPIRATIONS FROM WALES

Edited by

David Foskett

First published in Great Britain in 1996 by
ANCHOR BOOKS
1-2 Wainman Road, Woodston,
Peterborough, PE2 7BU

All Rights Reserved

Copyright Contributors 1996

HB ISBN 1 85930 313 7
SB ISBN 1 85930 318 8

Foreword

Anchor Books is a small press, established in 1992, with the aim of promoting readable poetry to as wide an audience as possible.

The poems in *Inspirations From Wales* represent a cross-section of style and content.

These poems are written by young and old alike, united in their passion for writing poetry.

I trust this selection will delight and please the authors from *Wales* and all those who enjoy reading poetry.

David Foskett
Editor

CONTENTS

A Tribute To Our Sons At Sea	G Chamberlain	1
Spring	Gladys Boorne	2
Untouched Snow	Rose E Selby	2
For My Sister	Susan Hollyman	3
New Moon	Michael Armitage	3
My Life	Alison Roberts	4
It's Too Late To Say 'Thank You'	N E Williams	4
Lament For Wales	R S Morgan	5
The Night Of The Storm	Daphne Thomas	6
New Day	Odysseus Ketchlove	6
Candles In The Rain	Norman Royal	7
Shooting Tears	Kevin Phelps	8
Untitled	Bernice Evans	9
Thought Of Spring	Vera Porter	10
A Winter's Thought	Glyn Eaton Butler	10
Isolation	Burton Richards	11
Hostage	J F Grainger	12
Touch Of Winter	Lisa Green	12
My Daydream	Mary Eileen Evans	13
Exhibitionist	Trak	14
A Strange Land	Phil Weber	15
Where Was The Blue Born?	Leah Edmunds	15
Dawn	Rhoda Lewis	16
The Silver Anniversary	Katie Feagan	16
The Ocean Of Life	Heather Paterson	17
A Prayer For Wales	Jean Parry	18
School Life 1940s	Margaret Bourne	19
Wonderful Spring	G M Ward	20
Rainbow	D James	20
Darkness	Marjorie Davies	21
Surveying The Land	P Thomas	22
Untitled	Siôn Hamilton	22
The Perfect Dream	G L Fenton	23

Instruments	Gareth Thomas	23
Dreams Of Ice	D Mack	24
A Happy Marriage	Catherine Rita May Lunt	24
The Essence Of Love	Mark Peter Evans	25
Pause	William Lowe	26
Semi-Detached - Or Don't Disturb The Neighbours	Myra Reeves	27
Soul's Guardian	Aileen Hopkins	28
September Song	Jan Roberts	28
Left To Carry On	Elizabeth Leach	29
Tree	Guy Fletcher	30
Together Forever	Michael Gerald Christy	30
Shattered Dreams	Odette Short	31
The House Up On The Hill	Gavin Mark Watkins	32
I Wonder . . .	Helen Walsh	32
Open The Gates Of Wales	Garrett John	33
Ode To North Wales	M Earles	34
Who Would A Tourist Be?	T S Jones	34
My Town	Dorrien Thomas	35
My World	Nancy Farr	36
Sonnet	Monica Traynor	37
Peace	George R Green	37
Bygone Glory	V Phillips	38
That's Why	Graham Jones	38
Tall Tales - A Gentle Story	Jean-Maria Lach	39
For Dunblane	Keith M Jones	40
My Mountain	Sally Moreton	41
The Tragedy Of Dunblane	Tabarna Young	42
Mothers' Tears	R P O Grady	43
Spring Again	E P Wood	44
If	T Benjafield	44
Peace	Hedydd Spencer	45
The Brock	J D Moyes	46
A Wondrous Place	Kenneth McDonald	46
Fred Hearse	Deborah Cowell	47
After Death	Carole O'Reilly	48

Face	Paula Stappleton	48
The Last Load		
Of Hay - Wrexham	Betty Glover	49
Aegina Reverie	David Price	49
Never Good-bye	Shirley Eastment	50
Mirrors Of The Soul	John Cowley	50
Global Walking	Catherine Brighton	51
Benson	Linda Roberts	52
In The Winter Meadow	Jane Hicks	53
Sonnet For Homework	Byron T Denning	53
My Cat	Danielle Jones	54
The Stream	Eric Hope	54
My County	Christopher Shaw	55
Windfarm	Anne Whitcombe Sterry	56
The Mouser	Louisa Diamond	56
Spiral	Andrew Archibald	57
Heartbreak And Hope	Carol Lewis	58
Autumn Wonder	G Gunter	59
The Witches' Cave	Amanda Iles	60
Hatred	Dariann S	61
My Land	Yvonne Lewis	61
Summer	V Hurford	62
My Street	Elizabeth Hughes	62
Unrequited Love	Rhian Prosser	63
Jigsaw	Barbara Hulse	63
Where The Artist Lives	Kath Wood	64
Children Of War	Carolyn McLeod	64
Dark Nights Of The Soul	George Colley	65
The Sunday Game	Julie A Kinnair	66
Let Nations Heed		
A Dreamer's Call	Gareth Lovell	67
Silence Of The Lamb	Lynden Tanner	68
Wales	Francis Allen	68
Delirium (For Selwyn)	Rhiannon Hart	69
Swimming	Stephanie Connors	70
God's Image	Frances Wright	70
Pit Closure	Catherine Mary Millard	71
War	Rebecca Hurle	72

White Satin	Joan Sayers	72
Michael	Anne Savan	73
Bygone Days	M L Cartwright	73
A Soldier's Farewell	Henry Ward	74
The South Western Wind	K Gmur	75
Soul Mate	E Bevan	75
Elin Mair	V Markham	76
Road Building	M M Watts	76
Drunken Venus	Kristian Evans	77
Woodlands Green	Arnold R Williams	77
The Lovers	Mark Dorey	78
Over The Rainbow	Rebecca Punter	78
Feelings Within	Julie Jones	79
The Price Of Coal - No 2	J A Edwards	80
To A Welsh Sheep Dog	Vera Parsonage	81
The Summer Of '41	Jean Davies	82
Gwent	R Miles	82
Waiting	T E Jeffery	83
A-Moosing - Cow's Eye View (*Bovine Sees Everything*)	Shelley Southwood-Clarke	84
My Valley, The Cynon	Gareth Hughes	85
Poblado Heights	A D Jones	86
A Cry To The Singing Wind	Hubert John Evans	86
Fergus	Celia G Thomas	87
True Love Waits	Kelly Davies	88
Mother's Heartache	Michelle Hughes	88
The Mountain Wall	R E Harper	89
Hope	Simon D Ford	90
Rhythm Chaser	Richard Lewis Cooke	91
They	P H Hunt	92
FA Cup Final 1996	Alan Jones	92
Castle	Jane Collins	93
Darkness	Mark Jones	94
God's Good Land	J A Parry	94
The Street I Loved	Christine Williams	95
Incomplete Heaven	Moira Lloyd	96
Forgotten Rhondda	C Evans	97

I Close My Eyes	W H Baghurst	98
Ode To Our Sweet Love (6 Yellow Roses)	G R Evans	98
The In-Laws	Christopher Herdman	99
Gwent	K Brown	100
An Exile's Return	Denise Jones	100
Will You Weep For The Children?	Nigel Power	101
The Rhondda Values	Kai Merriott	102
Metamorphosis	Lynda Newington	102
Perfection - A Lady	Michael Paul Ashcroft	103
War Kills	Suzanne Westwood	104
Music Of The Wind	Perter McNeil	104
My Sunshine	Helen Deborah Bennett	105
The Spirit Of Darkness	Diane Britton	106
I Had A Father You A Brother What A Man	Freda Biggs	107
More To Life	Helen Lewis	108
Untitled	Joe Waterman	108
The Bench	Karren Kinsey	109
Confusion	G Priest	110
Fallen Hero	Suzanne Swift	110
I Take No Prisoners	David L Brown	111
Goodbye Gwent	Meryl Anne Parfitt	112
Gwent	C McCarthy	113
Sheep Shearing 1940 Nantmel Radnorshire	William Austin Pugh	114
Beautiful Gwent	Sian Williams	115
My Happy World	Stephanie Jenkins	116
Remember	T R Llewellyn	117
The Mighty Heart Of Wales	Leanne Chapman	118
Gothic Romance	Paul Megycks	118
The Rainbow Fields	David Vaughan Lewis	119
My Unsung Hero	Elsie M Boyle	120
Loneliness	Clare Louise Mcdonald	121
Swimming	Anne Goulbourne	121
Eternity Is Like Tomorrow	Paul G Davies	122
Summer '95	Bernard Williams	123

Life	Joyce E Williams	124
The Welshman	Vikki Powell	124
City	G Elvira	125
All Quiet Now	Roy Wyatt	126
The Dragon	Thomas John West	127
Winter	E M Davies	128
The Garden's Call	Iris Puxty	128
Winter Scene	Margaret Coleman	129
A Special Wish	N G England	130
Too Late	J M Dickinson	131
Memories	Jane Lewis	132
Falling In Love	Craig A Leach	132
Caring	Margaret Jones	133
Snake	David Haydn Smith	134
First Born	Pamela Dawes	135
I Wonder Why	R Llewellyn	136
Seeing You Through	C Alun Jones	136
Springtime	N D Davies	137
Living Memory	M C Lawrence	138
Golden Days	Nick Purchase	138
Hiraeth	Sandie Page	139
Remembering	Ruth Lewis	140
A Blind Man In April	Peter Varley	140
Untitled	A Webley-Parry	141
Extinction	Emma Curtis	142
To The Future Of The Past	Karen Ann Grady	142
Little One	Linda Williams	143
The Volunteer	R B Douglas	144
Love's Hurt	Margaret Cave	144
Still C Of E . . . But Now, PLC	Wm Paul McDermott	145
Mother's Joy	Gaynor Davies	146
She's Starting Off For School	A Horton	146
Spirit And Stone	R E Sharp	147
Sad	Charles Wright	148
The Japanese Garden	David Madeira-Cole	148
Home At Last	Jill Munday	149
How Could I Help Myself?	Claire Frost	150

The Man	S W Coombes	151
Holidays!	Nikki Morgan	152
Reflections	V A Bater	152
Dragon In The Sky	Avril Williams	153
Earth	Wendall Stone	154
My Valley	Kaeleigh McGuire	155
The Beckoning	Janice	156
I Love You Forever And A Day	L A Brown	157
If I Was Never Born	A G Pengelly	158
Midnight In Misery	James Heaton	159
Acquired Memories	Lyn Thomas	160
Redundancy	Christine C Jones	161
Oak Tree	S M West	162
Where Herons Wade	Charles Ivor Morris	163
Animal Lovers	B G Waller	164
Wednesday	I Waller	165
Friendship	Tina Taylor	166
The Lonely People	Tina Simpson	167
Shadows Of The Fire	Sas	168
The Crystal	J D A Tickle	169
Fires In The Close	Paul Kearns	170
Winter's Edge Snowcrust At Owl Dusk	Neville Carlton	171
My Friend From The Sky	Helen Newman	172
To A Tree	Joanne Lavender	173
Diana	David Price Edwards	174
Symphony Of Voices (Curse Of Schizophrenia)	Sue Butcher	175

A TRIBUTE TO OUR SONS AT SEA

These boys, who have the call of the sea in their blood,
Are watched over, and taken care of by our Lord above,
The many tasks done by these *sailors* are told,
Although high waves may lash over their ship's side, and strong gales
may blow,
Still their strong strength of duty prevails, and their sense of humour and
wit still flows.

What breed of men are these? *All these sons of the sea?*
Did not Jesus say, in those days long, long ago?
'Those that go down to the sea in ships, and keep their faith in me
I shall be with each one of them, when their ships are pounded by the
cruel sea,
They shall remember that I the Lord have the power to walk on, and calm,
the waves'
All these boys clad in blue and white, with hearts that are stout and brave,
Even those whose caps are decorated by bands that are edged with gold
braid.

Their wisdom is given to them from the *Greatest Fisherman* of old,
One who never gave up, in the hope of capturing a man's soul,
Even when ships in distress, and prayers are sent out from the heart,
God hears each one and whispers 'Never fear, I will always do my part.

For those who have put their trust in me, and in my Faith believe,
The glory and praise due to them, I promise they will receive
For when their ship reaches my Heavenly shore, and that day will surely
come,
I will say I am well pleased with you and the deeds that you have done.'
What greater words could ever be said, with such a wealth of love?
Than those of our *Heavenly Father*, who dwells above,
Whose name stands forever and means *Perfect Love.*

G Chamberlain

SPRING

Primroses gleam in the hedgerows
Where sweet violets shyly peep,
Buds are bursting,
Birds are nesting -
Has winter gone to sleep?

Soon the clusters of blossoms
On may and apple trees decked,
Adorning their branches with beauty,
Catkins are yellow flecked.

Yes! Winter has flown,
No longer reigning
With its stern winds and snow,
Welcome spring, you lovely thing -
Come, gladden our hearts once more.

Gladys Boorne

UNTOUCHED SNOW

How lovely to see -
The snow covered ground,
That hasn't been touched -
'Cos there's no-one around.
No animals, no humans,
No footprints - no tread -
On the snow that has fallen
Whilst I was in bed.
How pretty the trees -
That are all dressed in white,
With the snow that has fallen
So silently at night.

Rose E Selby

FOR MY SISTER

Do I recall an older face
A voice to put me in my place
A teasing laugh, a wicked grin
A hand to put my own hand in.

Do I recall our secret ways
A piggy back on stormy days
The baggy socks, the frilly skirts
A gentle hand placed when it hurts.

Do I recall as things unfurl
From nursery child, to married girl
The times that we had all the fun
These forty years, they seem like one.

Do I recall a kindly word
When no-one else seems to have heard
Do I recall the very best
The answer now of course is, yes.

Susan Hollyman

NEW MOON

There was a new moon,
The spring grass was lush,
The west wind whispered
A mild muted hush.
They crossed the field
And climbed an old gate
It was cold and damp and already late.
They held each other close,
And closer still more -
Children of Nature,
Obeying Her law.

Michael Armitage

MY LIFE

Thoughts of joy and sadness
My life of utter madness
Times that have come and gone
So often I've been alone.

With memories linked together
The storm I've had to weather
Good chances I've rejected
Wrong paths I've then selected.

No point in backward glances
No more taking chances
The time has come to decide
I must face the world not hide.

Alison Roberts

IT'S TOO LATE TO SAY 'THANK YOU'

Friends of old of years gone past
Fade in reality but the memories last.
By gone days when life was more fun
Those glorious days spent lazing in the sun.
Dreaming of what the future may hold
Knowing everything without being told.
The boys you met along the way
Came and went but in your mind they stay.
Your lives took you in different directions
Along the way you made different selections.
The friendship you had you think is forgotten
Until life deals one of you a card which is rotten.
And so it's too late to thank that friend
For the friendship and memories you'll keep to your end.

N E Williams

LAMENT FOR WALES

The green grass has wither'd,
The mountains are bare,
The fox from the height slowly slinks to his lair,
But still through the stillness
Of Taff passing by
'Cymru am Byth!' seem the ripples to cry.

The blue sky has darken'd,
The streamlets are dry,
The hawk droops the wing and seems powerless to fly,
But still through the valleys
A whisper draws out,
'Cymru am Byth!' the vales seem to shout.

The trees grow in silence,
The crags stand mute;
Gone are the stains of the harp and the lute;
But still through the branches
A small voice sings,
'Cymru am Byth!' in the whirring of wings.

Our great Prince has vanish'd
His flower is dead;
Not a cheer is raised or a tear is shed;
But still in the darkness
Of death's vast hall,
'Cymru am Byth!' he still seems to call.

The call shall remain unanswer'd,
(Tho' hearts shall bleed!)
The daffodil in all her glory bows to the weed;
For now in the valleys
And mountain tops high,
'Cymru am Byth!' (Only the winds do cry!)

R S Morgan

THE NIGHT OF THE STORM

At
First it
Started with
A pouting puff,
Playfully prancing
And prettily pouncing.
Speeding up with a hurried huff
Hectic, howling, hissing, hurling,
Hustling, hasty, heralding havoc,
But direction changed and it grew gruff
Grumbling, growling, grizzling, getting gustier,
A gyrating, grappling, grabbing, grasping giant.
Then suddenly the tempest was not so tough,
Tossing, tangling, tensing, towsling, twining
Tentative, twittering, trembling
Regretting it had been too rough
Rummaging, rustling, roaming,
Roguishly relenting
Almost as if it
Had done enough
Suddenly
It had
Gone.

Daphne Thomas

NEW DAY

In our darkness we are like children
Not yet bestowed the gift of understanding
With defective eyes we see the imperfect world
And goad our concept into windowless towers
Casting shadows from the morning sun
Over the summer meadows of our waking

Arriving, to be transformed on love's winged freedom
Migrating hearts through fickle dimension
Thoughts memory not lingering to be remembered
To dance the destination of the eternal within
As each new day becomes *this life*
And breath becomes a gift from a king.

Odysseus Ketchlove

CANDLES IN THE RAIN

Hold fast the moment
of a passing sun,
for the sooner
the moment comes
then the sooner
it is gone,
just to out
like a candle in the rain

Hold close to you
the better day,
of the peachy dream
and ice-cream skies,
with both hands
to your heart,
for the moment
may never come again

And don't let go the moment
until you feel,
the very heartbeat inside
answering to the recall,
and feel the burning missing
from deep down within
the dark and inaccessible places,
that lie without the flame.

Norman Royal

SHOOTING TEARS

Why are you crying, Moon?

O, my light is sombre sad
And no brightness will outpour
My eyes are broken, old;
Not silvery grey or gold.
And soon to the depths of dark I die.

But Moon, my friend,
You cry too soon
For we all marvel at you
Your golden majesty fills the sky
And a purest charm shines through.

You can cut the dark
And make it bleed
Like silvery liquid flowing.
You are the beauty of the night
With diamonds around you growing.
Your cool breath is the Milky Way
And the silent stars your children.
You are a penny dropped from Heaven
To be never spent again.

So come now, dry your eyes
Smile for me, my friend, I say
And turn your tears to shooting stars
And send them far away.

Kevin Phelps

UNTITLED

Is my life over, or just begun?
Divorced, two kids, a *single mum*
Now it's just me and my two boys
Me in a daydream, them playing with toys
I only visit reality
With 'Mum, he's being nasty to me'
Now they're asleep, I escape once more
Inside my mind, a little trap door
Once opened, I meet him again
He's so unlike most other men
He's honest, caring and he loves me
For always, ever, eternity
He also loves both my boys
For all their moods, with all their noise
He's faceless, nameless, but I don't mind
Because he is good, because he is kind
I have met men who've looked at me
And could tell by their faces, they like what they see
And when they ask me 'What do you do?'
Lose interest when answered 'Mother of two'
I watch all the men I meet hesitate
For my boys to grow up, I'll just have to wait
As the boys and I equal three, not one
And this as you know can stop a man's fun
For now, I guess, my life is on hold
Unless the man of my dreams, I behold.

Bernice Evans

THOUGHT OF SPRING

Peeping over my window sill
I saw a single daffodil,
It spoke of spring, I felt a thrill
To see this flower above my sill.

I dressed and went outside to see
What else spring had in store for me,
Half hidden there beneath a tree
Two snowdrops, as if greeting me.

Upon my lilac tree once bare
Some sweet new buds were clearly there,
And as I breathed the dew-fresh air
I thought of spring as I stood there.

Vera Porter

A WINTER'S THOUGHT

The wind is keen
The sky's all grey
Will it snow? Who's to say.
Wildlife seems not to be found
As leaves blow across the hardened ground.
Some trees stand bare, tall and still,
Birds pass through them at their will.

People venture so quick and bold,
Others huddle from the cold.
Shadows cast from buildings lean,
All these things are a winter's scene.
We look through windows without a mime,
Dreaming of warm blue skies in summertime.

Glyn Eaton Butler

ISOLATION

Paranoia prevails in the darkness of your mind,
As you sit on the edge.
Watching yourself play the part
Like a puppet unaccustomed to the stage on which it performs.
Familiar faces at arm's length.
You're trapped in a tormented barrier of silence,
Self-inflicted systematic seclusion.
Everything you see is blurred and obscure,
Everything you want seems impossible to achieve.
No-one to talk to.
Unable to communicate,
Even though you want to say hello.
When everyone has a friend to turn to and you don't.
You're the odd one out,
The constant topic of private conversation.
When civilisation doesn't seem so civil.
And you're continually alienated,
All alone when you need someone to talk to.
Permanent solitary confinement.
When the relentless cold shoulder never seems to thaw.
Your cries for help ignored.
Leaving you rejected - a recluse.
Your self-esteem shrinking every minute.
When your every move is an unanswerable question
And your life has no meaning.
Insignificantly there.
Everything wrong,
Nothing right,
When you're uncertain,
When you're alone.

Burton Richards

HOSTAGE

My kidnappers were asking questions that were impossible to tell
I said to them why have me locked up in this vile prison cell
There I sit so afraid in the blackness without a single light
I couldn't tell was it daytime, or was it the middle of the night

I am so sacred and bewildered behind those strong steel doors
Thro' a hidden flap my food was pushed across the dirty floor
There I shivered with great fear my unclothed body is growing cold
My faith now lies broken and my courage has been cheaply sold

They bind my invisible wounds with those strong ugly chains
My feelings are so confused as they continue to invade my brains
There is no bed to lie on, I sit upon the floor because there's no seat
They took off my shoes and socks that once adorned my naked feet

Will my untimely death swiftly bring an end to the living hell
When they carry my wounded and broken body away from my evil cell
I won't cry, or be so afraid in the blackness without a light
To my kidnappers I say my last farewell, peace has come to me tonight

J F Grainger

TOUCH OF WINTER

Frosty mist forms a ghost-like beauty.
Distant trees and fields unreal.
Mountain top has merged with cloud,
becoming mystical I feel.

Colours dimmed and merged to grey.
Invisible farms with bleating sheep.
So cold and strange but wonderful.
The vision of it all is a land at sleep.

Velvet blackbird with striking bill
Foregoing in mangled undergrowth unseen.
Tangled web of brambles, of ivy.
But still the gorse is green.

Icy ponds and trickling brooks
and the leaves on the trees trodden back into earth.
Ginger ferns and yellow grasses
all waiting for spring's rebirth.

Lisa Geen

MY DAYDREAM

My day begins with feeding my man
Getting him off to work on time, if I can
Calling the kids up, in time for school
Being on time, for me, is a golden rule
Time is a factor so important in life
Yet the clock ticks on, in between each strike
As each hour chimes, meaning one less, I sigh
Before my time is up, and it's my turn to die
But why should I worry about things unforeseen
When I've shopping to do, and the house to clean
Really, washing, ironing, cooking and such
Doesn't give me time for worrying about much
As to how the country is being run without me
Being a member of Parliament is my big dream, you see
I would give all the housewives the rise they deserve
For the guts they've got, and having the nerve
To do all the things that are expected of them
Yes - they are the ones who stand at the helm.

Mary Eileen Evans

EXHIBITIONIST

You thought you were conceited
But now you think you're perfect
How on earth can you live
With all this raging conflict

You're the talk of the town
But you act like a clown
You're swank when you stagger
From the pub to your home

Your talk is cheap
All your friends fall asleep
They don't want to hear the stories
Of how you think you're so sweet

You think that God has gifted you
As something bold
You think your life won't end
You'll never grow old

Your insubstantial vain pride
Won't let you catch cold
But there comes a time
When you will be told

I just can't stand it
When you keep having your way
You're your own idol
The actor and the pop star

Can you leave your ego behind
Or will it keep catching up to you
Will you dream your life away
Thinking good things that you can do

Trak

A STRANGE LAND

I was taken one morning, at first light,
By a four winged bird, on a fantastic flight.
It carried me far, to a nest so high,
I reached out my hand, to touch a marshmallow sky.
There were green butter mountains in this strange land,
With a shaving foam sea and mercury sand.
Every blade of grass was a different hue,
All the flowers were a tartan pink and blue.
Houses were built out of copper or brass,
The trees that grew were of coloured glass.
Black stars shone in the light of day,
With cotton wool clouds surrounded with May.
There were no people, just china clay squares,
Rubber glass tables with flexible chairs.
Cups and saucers ran round on legs,
The birds all laid prismatic like eggs.
A beautiful fantasy, a mirage it did seem,
For it all disappeared at the end of my dream.

Phil Weber

WHERE WAS THE BLUE BORN?

Blue was it born in ice?
Blue was it born in Arctic winds?
Think deep and think
What's blue?
I know but do you?
Just think when it's rained,
When you wake up fresh
Sleepy when everything's wet,
In the November rains
That's how blue was born!

Leah Edmunds (10)

DAWN

Now the night will light and brighten
Up the sky with brilliant hues.
Gone the long prolonged darkness,
Once again the day is new.
New as a brand new button,
All shiny, shimmering sheens
Of deepest blues and emerald greens.

Rhoda Lewis

THE SILVER ANNIVERSARY

A silver sword catches the light,
A radiant eagle preys in the night.

Silver coins rattle in the hand,
Cold silver water on bleached silver sand.

An aeroplane, shining, leaves a trail,
The winding silver pathway of a snail.

Four calling birds in a Christmas song,
A Chinese man strikes a silver gong.

A silver tabby in a frolicsome mood,
Silver cling-film over mouth-watering food.

Silver ice on lush green grass,
A silent still pond just like glass.

Silver tears that show despair,
Silver fireworks throw silver flare.

Something forever, staying alive,
A silver anniversary of years twenty-five.

Katie Feagan (13)

THE OCEAN OF LIFE

Life is but an ocean full of waves.
Calmness and serenity - only on the still nights of summer.
Stormy, rough and loud; violent and boisterous,
like the delinquents of winter, who rule our lives
with playground torture - through the dark days of our lives.

The ocean can hurt, harm and destroy us,
but so rich with salt can cleanse our wounds;
deep the pores of thought,
soiled, dirty, discoloured - the stains of life.
Purest water of the clearest white may starch our minds from Hell.

So vast the ocean of life; such beauty a decade of waves;
such change upon reaching its shore.
So quick to die - the wave of time,
from blue to green to grey to white; as the ocean's years
roll on to sand - whose grains can count our life in days.

So free to swim the waters deep - the organs of our love.
To test its warmth and test its strength; our bodies ready
in deliberation anticipation; prepared to conceive its waters clear.
No untainted innocence - the soul's heart,
with breathtaking beauty - its springtime of grace.

The ocean's salt - now buoyant and strong; ready to carry
the weight of our tears. To sew together the heart of our lives,
so nearly drowned and cast away; as the tide came in
to meet the sand, the winter of our lives -
its grains to count; the salt no more.

Thinned out the ocean, its white to bare,
to mark the path its decades end.
The lesson learned; our souls prepared
for ever warmth, the desert to be;
the calmer life - *eternity*.

Heather Paterson

A PRAYER FOR WALES

A prayer for my homeland, where once my ancestors roamed
in the mountains and valleys of the green land of home.
I gives thanks for its beauty, of its hills and vales
in this much loved country, my homeland of Wales.

It's a land full of scenery, is our land of song,
and of harp and choir, it's where I belong.
Its beauty surrounds me, as each day I see
the farm lands and forestry, God given for thee.

A prayer for the people of this Welsh land,
for the spirit in communities, that now lie in our hands.
For the good Lord to guide us, in doing what's best
for our homeland, and its people, and for you Lord to bless.

I think of the homeless, seen every day,
may your church be there, in service I pray.
For all the unloved in Wales today,
may we show them your love, in a special way.

A prayer for this land, known for its songs,
let it also be known for righting its wrongs.
Please bring your love to Wales again
and your care to this land of misty rains.

My prayers and my thanks, I earnestly give
for all friends and family, in this land where we live.
In the beautiful country of mountain and vale.
It's a prayer from the heart, for my homeland of Wales.

Jean Parry

SCHOOL LIFE 1940S

James and Jimmy were school friends,
They shared a desk at the back
Of a class of 40 pupils
Their teacher a black country lass.

Their eyes were as bright as their minds
They hung on each word she said.
'Work hard and you'll both succeed,'
On words of equality fed.

James went home to his semi
With his room full of books.
Jimmy went home to his back to back
With its bookless, noisy, nooks.

They both worked hard each evening
Without cajoling or fuss.
They both achieved that elusive goal,
Both pass the eleven plus.

James' eyes reflected his parents' joy,
Jimmy's eyes his parents' worry.
For they couldn't fund his great success,
A poor family, short of money.

James went on to that hallowed place,
The local Grammar school.
While Jimmy swelled that other lot
The Secondary Modern school.

Disillusioned Jimmy went on to study
Many a frothy pint.
While that privileged lad from the suburbs
Enjoyed a most comfortable life.

Margaret Bourne

WONDERFUL SPRING

Spring is here, with its clear blue skies
Fresh is the air now winter dies.
Hibernators begin to open their eyes,
To see they get food, so to survive.
Spring creeps in on tippy toe,
As if she doesn't want you to know.
A quick glance at the seedling show,
It's on the way, but ever so slow.
How wonderful nature is, it's said,
When you see a flower raise its head.
The seeds pop their heads above the ground
Including the weeds, are to be found.
Now that the ground is getting warmer,
A bumper crop, I hope, and wonder.
The thunder, lightning, rain and wind
Rainbows, and robins on the wing.
Greenfly, slugs and snails arrive
With the spring they will all come alive.
When spring has come and passed once more
When fruit and flowers begin to fall,
We will soon be back to the winter again
But, spring will be back with all its flame
Spring is the time of giving new life
Which brings its glory to all the earth.

G M Ward

RAINBOW

There's a rainbow in my garden, and the rain is pouring down
We haven't had much winter, but spring has spread her gown.
Daffodils yellow, being swayed by the rain,
Snowdrops, pure white, raise their head, oh so vain,
Heathers, rich heathers, a soft rosy pink, clustered
Together, forming a link, with the evergreen shrubs and their
                                              tracings of gold
  Sheltering small tulips, red colour so bold.

Primroses, cowslips, pale lemon hue
Delicate vinca, purple and blue
Magical colours offset with green,
Form a rainbow of beauty, a sight to be seen.

D James

DARKNESS

God saw a raging ocean
Engulfed in black darkness,
And said, 'Let there be light.'
Then all became brightness;
His work of creation
Began.

God did not discard darkness,
But separated it
From light, which He called, 'Day' . . .
Then, used, as He saw fit,
The dark to bring earth rest.
At night.

The darkness could not hinder
God's plan, or shake His might;
Heralded by sunset,
The daylight turned to night
Until, in splendour broke
The dawn.

Sunset and dawn are certain,
For, darkness God o'ercame.
In life's darkest moments
Just breathe His holy name.
Trust Him. The sun will shine
Again.

Marjorie Davies

SURVEYING THE LAND

April morning, light is dawning.
Haze in the sky, but the land is dry
No time to waste, must make haste.
Out in the garden, the sun has come out
Birds are singing and feeding about
The lambs are crying, in the meadow below
A touch of frost, but no sign of snow.

Ancient woods, I love the best
But now machines, have made a mess
Torn down trees, such as oaks
I think progress is no joke
Wild primrose has gone, wild orchids too,
Oh, how I cry what they are doing to you.

Children of the future protect your rights
I find it hard to sleep at nights
Protesters, try so hard to be heard
And still progress has the last word.
All is not lost, within this land.
People have to make a stand
Thousand trees to be felled at will
Just so progress, does not stand still.

P Thomas

I lie
    Prostrate
        Before God.
Then the thought -
She's dead.
Her death gives birth to sorrow,
Sorrow fills the gap she's left.

Siôn Hamilton

THE PERFECT DREAM

Dream of the world alive and living.
With each person reacting and corresponding as they should.
Black and white: every colour being true.
Green and pink it does not matter.

Perfect equality.

Dream of the world: living and breathing.
Each person knowing and caring.
Nationality next to nationality: every word correct
Systematically and perfectly in rhyme,
Technically uncriticisable.

Dream of the world: realistically and idealistically
Each person running parallel, in harmony.

No more wars, no more bloodshed,
No disease, no fatality.

People by people
The perfect dream: when time can say,
'No dreamers!'

G L Fenton

INSTRUMENTS

Oh instrument of time and instrument of space,
an instrument of eternity that cannot be erased.
You're an instrument of fools and an instrument of hate,
an instrument of poetry that captures time and space.
Oh instrument of peace, oh instrument of grace,
just like the solar winds that flow through time and space,
that brush our planet's landscape that's scarred and filled with hate.
The dawning of a new age, the dawning of our fate,
is held within our hands and the solar winds of space.

Gareth Thomas

DREAMS OF ICE

Look at life with narrowed view,
Not dreams, but reality to pursue.
Wishes shatter like winter ice,
You can't buy hopes at any price.

So, only look at what is real,
The things that influence how you feel.
Scrutinise the true facts of life,
Take the pain of an honest knife.

Cut away the things you want,
Reality is the prize to hunt.
Leave the emotions free to choose
A path not clouded by gilded ruse.

Beware, one moment all the world seems right,
But next, the future has gone from sight.
The hopes and visions that you see,
Without real substance, dissolve and flee.

D Mack

A HAPPY MARRIAGE

Marriage is a partnership, enter it with care
The good times and the bad times, are things you both must share
There are times you will feel tired, and small things get you down
Talk about your problems, don't sulk and cry and frown

With a little understanding, and with lots of love you'll find
You both will be rewarded with a happier frame of mind
When your family starts to grow, a girl and then a boy
You will have your share of worries, and lots of love and joy

You will need a lot of patience as they reach their teenage years
With lots of love and guidance, to help them through their fears
Be friends as well as parents, have trust in one another
And they will have respect for you, their father and their mother

And as you both grow older and the children leave the nest
There'll be no need for reproaches, you will know you've done your best
Then think of all the happy times, and some times that were sad
When you look back you'll thank the Lord for the good life that you have
                                                                                          had.

Catherine Rita May Lunt

THE ESSENCE OF LOVE

The days are long the nights are cold
The forgotten times can only diminish and unfold
Charms that express love in many ways,
Behold the love that grows day by day,

The beam that entwines from your eyes, your smile,
Shines the light memories that last and last throughout the night
So near so far so short so long
The waiting to see you just prolongs,
The innocence that delves from the utmost of all unnatural things
Remind the world and its people of the echoes of closeness that
Togetherness brings,

The heart that delivers such a tiny beat
The hand that wears the glove,
Only reminds the stars of true true love,

Being as two being as one, is the part that nothing can break
Love is special love is kind like a separate whisper that gathers no hate.

Sun and moon wind and rain snow and frost
Together forever brings forth that love can, never be lost . . .

Mark Peter Evans

PAUSE

Soft whispers in the night sky
Underneath the moon I lie
My heart stops, I understand
When substance turns to sand
Counting all the stars in sight
Feeding off celestial light

I close my eyes, the view remains
Taking deep emotional pains
A million points of fire
Seems to give me a desire
For life, my hunger mounts
Removing all my doubts

This sight makes me want to sleep
Questions I ask seem so deep
And meaningful, with hidden truths
What will become of today's youths
Earth of the future's ours
In what ways will we use these powers

Air I breathe condensates
I ponder over my fate
What shall become of me
Will I roam these worlds free
Beauty lifts my heart
With everything, I become part

At last I feel true love
Warmth radiates from above
Letting out a solemn sigh
All questions are answered concerning my life

William Lowe

SEMI-DETACHED - OR DON'T DISTURB THE NEIGHBOURS

Once,
in a far-off stone-sheltered house,
we could make music to our hearts' content,
quarrel, shout, laugh, or even practice singing,
and no one heard.

Now, the rustle of curtains
drawn wide to welcome golden light
breaks the silence of early day.

Does it wake the sleeping neighbours
on the other side of the wall?

Even birds are muted
after their first sky-flung exultant joy.

Through the window
drifts the sweet dew-drenched air,
fresh as summer fields.
Breathe deep of the dawn . . .
but quietly!

Once it was possible to lean far out
listening to steeple bells about this hour
thrown from the tower less than a thought away.

Now, soften the radio voice:
'Commandos are surrounding
the Golden temple of Amritsur.'

Britain deplores violence,
but does it circumspectly,
treading delicately,
not to disturb her transatlantic neighbour.

Myra Reeves

SOUL'S GUARDIAN

You stepped into a lightness clear
when you edged but into view,
As ne'er once had I felt so near
to any as loved but few,
But once you set your gaze on me
the sweet guardian to my soul,
Drew back to let your eyes so be
all entwined with mine in roll.

My being dwelt deep in repose
but you then imposed upon,
So the guardian to my soul arose
all to let your light shine on,
My upturned face with moist lips set
to partake of love's sweet kiss,
And feel your soft touch as to let
my heart soar in pleasured bliss.

But the wise guardian knew true
what my eyes fain would not see,
That the veneer which mantled you
was not purely right for me,
As 'twas not a true reflection
of your inner strength and soul,
When the art was in deception
and the guardian saw the whole.

Aileen Hopkins

SEPTEMBER SONG

Late love is ruthless
An overwhelming tide
Past sense and beyond reason
It sweeps old ways aside.

Late love is ruthless,
For autumn winds, though chill,
Fan up glowing embers
To volcanic passion still.

    Yes, late love is ruthless
        and cannot be denied.

Jan Roberts

LEFT TO CARRY ON

I go over everything in my head
I pray to God and go to bed
I don't understand the things you do
And all you think of is just you
You don't come to see us anymore
You don't bother to knock upon our door
I suppose this is a way of saying to me
This is the way you want it to be
You are just getting on with your life now
How we survive I don't know how
You never even said goodbye
It's just as well I'd only cry
That is all I ever seem to do
Whenever I think or see you
I don't understand how you can turn away
Because once again you make us pay
We're not at fault for what you do
Why can't you think of anyone but you
You don't stop loving or caring you see
Just because you want it to be
It's easy for you to carry on
Doing the things that are so very wrong
I'll never stop hurting over you
As long as you do the things that you do.

Elizabeth Leach

TREE

We are like the tree which stands on the barren hill,
Battered and beaten by the torturing wind,
Bent like an old man, suffering until
It finally blows down, then eternal rest it'll find.
Now is the time for sad reflection,
To play life's movie, to see ghost after ghost,
A few islands of joy on the sea of dejection.
Oh, she is the one whom I miss the most.
The sun shines through only once in a while,
The dark clouds of fate weigh us down.
Soft lips at dawn, a willing smile,
But now she has gone and I must walk on my own.
I am like the tree which stands on the barren hill,
Longing for the tormenting wind to be finally still.

Guy Fletcher

TOGETHER FOREVER

Step by step
Your love will bind
Opening up your hidden mind
A feeling - A touch
You can never ignore
Like a shell that swept upon the shore
It left its mark
It left its trail
With love like that you'll never fail
And now you'll wed
And live your life
Together forever
Like man and wife

Michael Gerald Christy

SHATTERED DREAMS

I didn't ask for love
But you gave it to me
I didn't ask for dreams
But they followed
I didn't ask for promises
And hopes of better living
I didn't ask for anything
But still you kept on giving
And now I ask myself
Can love really be true?
What I mean to say is
Was it love
This thing between me and you
When I accepted you
Or should I say loved you
You threw it in my face
You watched me bury my pride
And let my heart give chase
I thought once that two people
Were meant for each other
And when I loved you
You would love me
Oh! What a fool I must have been
To let you bring such misery
I didn't ask for love
I didn't ask for emptiness
I gave no cause for you to leave
And shatter dreams of hopefulness
But now I'll live without you
And hope true love will come
Fulfil my shattered dreams
And let me live to love again.

Odette Short

THE HOUSE UP ON THE HILL

An empty bottle of gin
A pill bottle.
Watching a sad 50's movie on TV
Left there, discarded
Unwanted.

She lay there motionless
As she had for the past hour.
No-one would find her for many more.
No one knew her, except in fleeting.
So lonely on her own,
In the house up on the hill.

No-one really cared or talked about it much,
Warnings were given, but none were truly heeded.
The same fate always fell upon
All those who lived up there,
In the house up on the hill.

For sale again, boarded windows,
Vacant rooms not quite empty.
Another has joined the numbers
In the house up on the hill . . .

Gavin Mark Watkins

I WONDER . . .

As I sit here all alone, no sound, no ringing of the phone,
I think of the world - how long will it last?
And of all the things that have happened in the past.
I think of my life now, and what has happened to me.
I wonder what the future holds - I'll have to wait and see.
I wonder if, in my later years, there will ever be a war
And if the world will last - for evermore.

I wonder if the world will ever change that much.
Will people's hearts and minds be even harder to touch?
I wonder if nuclear weapons will stop being produced,
And will all these CFCs ever be reduced?
I wonder if there will be a time when total peace will exist,
Or will our troubles be included in a much longer list?

I wonder . . .

Helen Walsh

OPEN THE GATES OF WALES

Not a bridge too far, three traffic lanes out of Wales two traffic lanes in welcome to Wales once a dynasty of industry now being swallowed up by an evil tide.

Disaster the way of Welsh life, hymns of tears from days gone by should be a workplace for life, Welsh people prisoners in there own land the bounty hunters closed our industry down.

Where not people of impurity let the evil tide go out, open up a Welsh parliament let their voices speak out, the gift of nature now overgrown, only the Tower colliery stands alone.

The bounty hunters got it wrong the Tower colliery was too strong, lift our glasses to the men of Wales, the gift of nature stay with them.

Evil tide go away raise our voices to a Welsh parliament speak out for the people of Wales, use 'nature's' gifts for Wales open up the mines employ Welsh people again, make our country a tax haven, our own language must flourish again, sing a new hymn for Wales, take the tears away voices sing out Coal, Water, Oil, this will make Wales rich again, welcoming to the gates of Wales.

Garrett John

ODE TO NORTH WALES

To see the birds of the air
Soar over hills so fair
Oh to sit and admire the view
In places where you'd find no queue

There's lakeland, serene and blue
So many beauties of nature too
Wild flowers growing on the heath
With moss and lichen underneath

A place of peace to gaze awhile
With just the sheep for many a mile
A hillside farm tucked out of sight
No sound of traffic in the night

A haven for some though not for all
Some like to hear the curlew call
For some the lure of the city
For me the quiet tranquillity

M Earles

WHO WOULD A TOURIST BE?

Who would a tourist be?
Offer him no pity.
To many he's trash.
Kindly, just cash.

Who would a magistrate be?
Offer him no pity.
To many he's vile.
Kindly, just bile.

Who would a newspaperman be?
Offer him no pitee.
To many he's mutilate.
Kindly, just titillate.

Who would a teacher be?
Offer him no pity.
To many, he's pedagogue.
Kindly, just make a fog.

T S Jones

MY TOWN

The paving slabs are uneven and cracked,
they lead the way there and back.
The traffic it seems never ending,
Mail vans deliver what people are sending.
People mingle, pushing to and fro,
the traffic lights never seem to be on go.
Music from shops, it can be heard,
Understand it, no fear not a word.
Traffic Wardens move cars, which are not in the way.
Others that obstruct they let them stay.
I have been hours, walking around and around,
What I want to buy can never be found.
People stop and talk, it's like walking through a maze,
They are oblivious to you and your gaze.
Supermarket trolleys in every street,
A river which once sailed a fleet.
Merlin's oak once stood, now they have pulled it down
Myth said if it fell so would Carmarthen town
For all that was, has gone away,
Was the myth true? Who can say.

Dorrien Thomas

MY WORLD

A child growing up in the thirties
I played in the woods and the street
at skipping marbles and hop-scotch.
No cars just the patter of feet.

I went off to school on my own
came home with my best friend
no fear of being abducted
harming children wasn't the trend.

No television or computers
the radio was a treasure
for those who could afford it
others read a book for pleasure.

A holiday in August
flying off to Spain!
To Barry Island on the bus
was really my domain

The air was not polluted
the sea was really blue
no broken glass to cut my feet
some paper bags, a few.

For tea a suet pudding
or maybe apple pie
no junk food from the freezer
Mam made, she didn't buy.

My world it wasn't perfect
but I went to Sunday School
to learn about the love of God
and how true values rule.

Nancy Farr

SONNET

Look you through the light of night
Upon the dark of day;
I sing now not as Dylan sang,
But in a sober way.

The strutting cockerel heavenward slings
His silent serenade;
While she, coy hen, of plaster cast,
Will ever be a maid.

Of gaudy Portugal the sign
He, red and green, she brown,
beside the clock she clucks and frets,
And gets his tea on time.

Just so, replete, with Ovaltine I struggle with my prayers
At half-past ten I set the clock and make my way upstairs.

Monica Traynor

PEACE

Humanity gone, out the door.
Peaceful nations are no more
Nobody cares if you live or die
Always war and conflict, why.

Wracked in pain, numb of thought
This is what the conflicts brought
Lives are lost, but it's peace we yearn
Can you people ever learn.

Eyes of tears, cold with fear,
Starvation draws ever near
Hope is gone, nowhere to turn
Can you people ever learn.

George R Green

BYGONE GLORY

Storm clouds gather.
The castle gazes.
And remembers.
Each battle. Each victory. Each defeat.

Where is the king
Who stood upon the parapet
And cried defiance against the world?
Where are the warriors
Who unfurled the banner?

Children play in the crumbling tower.
Parents search and admonish them.
And by the keep
Where the prince was slain.
Stand a parking-place for cars.

V Phillips

THAT'S WHY

Sun splits the grey cloud, and through rain
Shines coldly through the window pane,
And just as cold and bleak does seem
This life of mine without love's dream.

Love's not a gift you can command,
Or steal it with a grasping hand,
Love only lives when given free
Love chained could never ever be.

That's why, my love I must let go,
And she must never ever know
My sorrow, and how deep my pain
When looking at the sun through rain.

Graham Jones

TALL TALES - A GENTLE STORY

Tall tales and tenuous footings
In verdant valleys
Above which rise bleak barriers
Havens of heath and heather.

Here tall tales are told
To troubled tempers
Whispered wordlessly,
Perhaps published
Privately.

Told is this tale
Of the orange striped cat.

What will that dear old man do
When his ancient and loved cat dies?

He dotes on her
She dotes on him.

We watch, worrying and waiting.
We want another cat. Why not?
Against that dreadful day.

Then, the old man dies,
And we, ha, we
Are *still*
Feeding the orange striped cat
And her replacement.

Such tenuous footings,
Such tall tales
Spring up in verdant valleys.

Jean-Maria Lach

FOR DUNBLANE

He carried it for sport
So said the news report
Just shooting pests his aim
Or targets in a frame

He went to school today
Where children learn and play
Oh God what's in his head
To leave so many dead

They say such men are few
If only it were true
For madness strikes so fast
But consequences last

Don't take away my fun
I have to own a gun
I need it on the farm
I'll keep it safe from harm

How can there be debate
For surely it's too late
And who can count the cost
The case for guns is lost

From truth you cannot hide
Nor hold your head in pride
A permit you unfurl
But they have lost their girl

We ask you in God's name
Why do you play this game
You stand to lose a gun
They've lost their only son

Please Parliament now vote
No gun shall people tote
The carnage at Dunblane
Must not be seen again

Keith M Jones

MY MOUNTAIN

I live 'neath a mountain, that's seamed to the sky
So beautiful its magic, it could've made a man cry,
for in a past age man ripped it apart
tunnelling deep in its innermost heart.
Now in this day and the mines are history
my beautiful mountain relives its glory.
Covered in forest, bracken, heather and moss
it's regained all its power from innermost loss.
I climb up my mountain and it gives me a feeling
of freedom and peace, or can I be dreaming
like an ant on an anthill soldiering on
a fox in the wood, cunning and strong.
My aim is the top where I'll stand and breathe deeply
the wonderful atmosphere capturing inside me,
the air is so fresh, clean and absolute
away from exhaust fumes and all that pollutes.
This natural elevation in our trusty land
pushes me gently towards heaven in its hand
and makes me respect life and living that's cherished
forgetting greed, wealth and wars and all that has blemished.
Like the sun I descend, leaving my heart,
but my thoughts on the summit, they will not part
and tomorrow as a bright new day's dawning,
I'll climb and rejoice on this brave land's forming.
Reunite once again my body and soul
become like my mountain, once again whole.

Sally Moreton

THE TRAGEDY OF DUNBLANE

Who's to say where this hatred ends,
The cold nasty shiver, that it sends.
Sixteen young children, lay peacefully dead,
Many a tear has already shed.
How can someone think of something so sick,
To get out of this, an unsightly kick.
Ending their lives, and then taking his own,
I hope hell's where he's at, sitting alone.
I feel for the families, of those angels above,
You can see in their face, a great loss of love.
The Queen arrived, and paid her respects,
A tear was shed, these are the affects.
Why so young - If at all?
In their own gym, or their sports hall,
Running around, avoiding shots
Barely aged, just out of cots.
Something must be done, to end this crime.
No more waiting or wasting precious time.
I send my condolences, to each one in grief,
And I hope your sadness, is very, very brief.
Although I know better, and thoughts do last,
But look at the future, and put away the past.
The accused is gone, and is away forever,
You've grieved alone, and grieved together.
Although he's unpunished, and won't be back,
Love and affection, is what he did lack.
I hope the children rest peacefully, and Gwenne Mayor too,
In her protection above, just awaiting for you!

Tabarna Young

MOTHERS' TEARS

One day my little grandson climbed up upon my knee
Saying granddad I've some questions for you to answer please
Is it true that God made everything the earth the sky and then
When he had finished making them he finally made men

Granddad you are old and wise so will you please explain
Did God really make them all and does he make the rain
Did he make the birds and fishes and all animals that run
He must be very clever to know how to work the sun

I answered that the bible tells God worked for six whole days
We can only wonder and praise God's wondrous ways
He made fathers sisters grandparents uncles aunts and brothers
But I know God worked a second week to make what we call mothers

This part of my answer absorb and understand
For God made all the things you said with one wave of his hand
He made this world of beauty he makes us clear blue skies
The only thing God doesn't make are tears in mothers' eyes.

You are just a little lad may you have what it takes
To listen to old folk like me and learn from our mistakes
Remember your old Granddad's words some day you'll realise
Why God would never claim to make the tears in mothers' eyes

These tears are made by children who on their way through life
Do foolish things and break the heart of the one who gave them life
They turn deaf ears to all her pleas they waste their youthful years
Add all these things together and they make
    Mothers' Tears

R P O Grady

SPRING AGAIN

The wintry winds and snow have gone
And little lambs have just been born
Daffodils, crocus and snowdrops too
Violets with their purple hue.

The blackbird and thrush begin to sing
As if to say it's not long till spring
When they will build their nests nearby
The sun will be shining way up high

And April will be here again
With all its sunshine and showering rain
Time for Easter Eggs and Hot-x-buns
And many happy days to come
So let's rejoice it's spring again.

E P Wood

IF

If wars were not invented
And people really cared,
The governments relented
And children never scared.
If black and white got together,
The hungry had their fill,
If people had employment
And man were taught not to kill.
Then perhaps our hearts would be lifted,
We could see the love for miles,
Everyone, everywhere would be gifted
And maybe we'd learn how to smile.
Maybe one day we will realise
And the hate may eventually cease,
A sun so golden will start to shine
For freedom, for laughter, for peace.

T Benjafield

PEACE

Stand up oh people of Ireland,
Stand up and show you believe,
You have suffered and mourned for too long
Too long you have been made to grieve.

March in the streets and shout loud.
Shout out and make them hear.
Those who are destroying your freedom,
Killing those you hold dear.

Why should this small group of die-hards
Destroy your much longed for peace?
Stand up together and tell them
That from them you want release.

Catholics and Protestants together
With hands linked should make their point clear
No more of the killing and mayhem
No more of the living in fear.

You are the people of Ireland
Whose power is at present deranged.
By marching together with hands joined
You can show them your courage to change.

Love one another as God says.
Desire destroys and just maims.
Power with love is the answer,
Show them you mean to change.

Take from them their means of destruction
By showing your numbers and strength.
By uniting together in love now
Your voice will be heard at length.

Hedydd Spencer

THE BROCK

Deep in his set
Away from light
Lies Mr Brock
Out of sight

Lays there safe
Lays there warm
Until comes
The crack of dawn

Footsteps break
The peaceful silence
Face to face
They fight with violence

Dog and brock
Out of breath
But this will not curve
The inevitable death
Of a black and white creature
Who lives deep in his set.

J D Moyes

A WONDROUS PLACE

There is another wondrous place
Over the stars amongst the heather
Where gentle breezes caress your face
And cares and worries have no place.

The sky is blue and rainbows abound
There is laughter and love all around.
Busy bumble bees make their honey
And I have no need of money.

In this paradise place I am
Young and without pain again.
The sun shines all day long
And angels sing their songs.

There I find you waiting for me
Along with all my family.
I hope to leave this tiring life
And live forever there with you my wife.

Kenneth McDonald

FRED HEARSE

When we were young we had a secret dread
it was a relation of ours called uncle Fred
he was completely obsessed with his chosen profession
which was totally gruesome and somewhat depressing
People who knew him called him Fred Hearse
But to us kids he was a terrible curse
for he'd take us for a ride on a Sunday afternoon
we'd sit in his car faces full of gloom
for we knew we'd end up in a crematorium
we used to call them all Fred's emporium
And then he'd insist on showing us all backstage
never had a man been happier earning his wage
but we never had sympathy from our mother
she'd say don't be unkind to your grandma's brother
he's kind to bring us dusters so soft and fine
it's only the expensive coffins they line
but Fred was happy doing his job
even though people he met would snivel and sob
and so Fred travelled the country for miles
his coffin behind him and his face full of smiles

Deborah Cowell

AFTER DEATH

Today I tread a new path through the yews,
a dance of lightning
whitewashed by rainbows.

My summer bouquet is hardening to wicker,
my porcelain veil
is whipped to a froth.

The red carpet wriggles to eject confetti
and threatens to
jam-roll the guests

O careless June your tree has wept
leaves on the altar,
tears on the grass.

The vicar's hi-lily hi-lo curdles the silence,
and a cough claps
like a thunderbolt.

Carole O'Reilly

FACE

A mask to hide the person inside
What emotion are you trying to hide
How much will you reveal
Maybe not as much as you feel
You can be a useful tool
Yes, for a vain fool
You can shine with so much beauty
But only to hide the ugly.
You are of course a work of art
With your root at the heart
Face, what are you concealing
As all you're doing is deceiving.

Paula Stappleton

THE LAST LOAD OF HAY - WREXHAM

Into the field the children came racing.
Along with their dogs the low swallows chasing.
Long summer days in freedom exalting.
Over the neat little hay stacks vaulting.
Now it's too dangerous for them to play.
Gone is the joy of a romp in the hay.

For centuries the noble horse did plod,
Where development now turns the fertile sod,
And where the children sang with merriment,
The builder starts to lay his base cement,
And brick, by brick, the brickies' bricks arise,
Where sky larks rose to bless the morning skies.

As the bright town lights bid Goodbye to day,
Our last load of hay is carried away,
And I stand and think in the scented twilight,
Of the people's problem, and the horses' plight
Space restricted children in childhood brief,
And the last harvest home is sensed with grief.

Betty Glover

AEGINA REVERIE

Nor will I again swim in the sea of despair
But rise above the problem to a greater height
Never again to wallow in self-doubt or pity
For the human spirit is alive and strong
Within the bounds of one's own mind.

David Price

NEVER GOOD-BYE

We stand on the platform as though we are strangers,
trying hard to cope with the torment going on inside.
I gaze at you longingly, memorising your loving face,
The warm, hazy breeze plays gently with your dark
curly hair as a silent tear escapes from my clouded eyes.
You reach out to hold me for one more time, the last time?
Your hand touches my face, raising it up towards your
lips, my heart beats so fast as though it's trying to
break out to be with you, as I wish I could be.
Your train arrives to take you away from me,
We don't know what to do, there are so many things to
say, we just stand there fingers entwined, staring
at each other. I know you have to go, but please
try to understand how I feel. I love you.
A tender smile creeps into your face, as you smother
me in your arms. I know you will be back in two days,
but it's so hard to say good-bye.

Shirley Eastment

MIRRORS OF THE SOUL

The lights I see they mean so much,
They caress my soul for it they touch.
Gentleness and tranquillity I feel,
So soothing yes, so very real.

My arms enfold you holding you near,
To me you are so very dear,
Your skin so soft your hair so fine,
I thank our God that you are mine.

Yes your pool-lit lights sparkle for me,
They cast out darkness their light is free.
Showing me that you are near,
O yes you are so very dear.

You take my hand we walk awhile,
As we stop, I catch your smile.
The lights I see have me in sighs
As they sparkle forth out of your eyes.

John Cowley

GLOBAL WALKING

Our Joke
To take the world for a walk
Hooked onto the pole
The leather leash threaded
Through the ozone hole
The friction against the space pavement
Burning Australia
The history trail
And the itched plains
Oh God! I'm but a nit
On a fur-tree coat
I hang about the mountain ears
And near to the throat
I feel the pull
On the metropolis collar
Ahead the nuclear nuzzle
And I worry
This dog can walk alone
This dog can walk alone

Catherine Brighton

BENSON

I miss you so much Ben old friend,
I thought those days would never end.
The times we'd walk for hours long,
I miss them so much now you're gone.

You loved to walk come rain or shine,
The weather wasn't always fine.
You sometimes liked to go alone,
In fact you'd sneak off on your own!

You were such a loving pal old lad,
You seemed to sense when I was sad
You'd peer at me with big brown eyes,
Ears cocked, to twice their size!

Then you'd start to wag your tail,
You knew I'd smile, it couldn't fail!
I loved you so much Ben old friend,
But fate stepped in, it had to end.

I think God chose you specially,
He loved you too, it had to be!
He couldn't stand to see your pain,
Nor your suffering in vain.

He took you home to make you well,
Release you from your painful shell
To let you once again be free,
Happy like you used to be.

Linda Roberts

IN THE WINTER MEADOW

In the winter meadow, cold grass stands pale
Stiffened with a deathly frost that stifles summer life.
Tall mourning weeds wear dimming colours, covered in a rough edged ice.
Trees stand withdrawn in summer dreams, bare in wood and spring
revealing bud.
Branches moved by careless winds sway unresisting in their sleeping state.
Lone birds fly in separating search, far above the winter field.
Wind driven, weather bound, bereft of summer grain,
They wheel and soar adrift in winter's song.
Tall meadow bounded trees grow pale behind the ice smoked air
And topmost branches brush the low grown cloud.
Burdened cloud that hangs, grey heavy with a fall of snow
That seeps in sifting dry froze grains to cover fallen leaves.
It falls to lie in unrelenting binding strength
And stills the land beneath its winter cloak.

Jane Hicks

SONNET FOR HOMEWORK

Unjust, unfair is your demand
To write a sonnet in a day,
And yet it's yours to make command
And just for us to make obey.
A topic now I have to choose.
Shall it be nature, art or love?
'Come to my aid, you lofty Muse!
Enthuse my soul from realms above.'
No use! My pen you can't inspire
To satisfy the English 'Miss'.
Alas! I find no bardic fire -
The Muse doth not my ball-point kiss.
Yet, 'spite it all, depend upon it -
I'll finish off this blasted sonnet!

Byron T Denning

MY CAT

Its ears tuned to a pin drop aware and listening,
in the moonlight he stands with his beady eyes glistening.
His sharp knife-like claws a dazzling white,
as he hunts his prey, a bird in flight.

Keeping himself tidy and grooming his fur,
he greets a lady cat with a heart-warming purr.
As he strolls down the alleyway his head held high with pride,
with great arrogance he takes each stride.

As fast as a bullet, he runs at tremendous speed,
rushing home for his early morning feed.
His claws in the bark he would engrave,
but then in his cosy basket he would sunbathe.

Chasing leaves in the garden he'd play,
and at night below the fire he'd be lay.
When his food arrives, in sink his razor teeth,
but when my food is served, where's the turkey? The thief!

Danielle Jones (12)

THE STREAM

High in the hills, there's a bubbling spring,
It spreads itself outward to do its own thing,
It forms its own channel, and as you look
It turns itself into a babbling brook.

It babbles away so peaceful and clear,
Running water is always a joy to hear,
So follow it gently, and then it would seem,
The brook has become a widening stream.

As you watch, it appears to be in a hurry,
Bursting round rocks in a white water flurry,
You see the birds drinking, and hear their calls,
Where the stream descends in steep waterfalls,

Then on down the hill, where it grows ever bigger,
To the end of its run in a fast flowing river,
And in its flight, it's wild and it's free,
Till at last it flows into the wide open sea . . .

Eric Hope

MY COUNTY

So much to do, so much to see,
My county is such a nice place to be,
There are seaside resorts, and mountains too,
And the River Dee, to paddle a canoe,
There are lots of villages, and plenty of towns,
But not one city, with its ups and downs,
In Deeside there is a large ice rink,
Buckley Tivoli nightclub will sell you a drink,
There are lots of castles, where battles were fought,
And in the north-east is Hawarden airport,
In Llangollen, there's the Horseshoe Pass,
Surrounded by hills, and lots of grass,
Wrexham have a league football team,
To get to the Premier League is their dream,
There is a country park at Loggerheads,
Where people walk and make slow treads,
My county is the gateway to Wales,
Clwyd it is, with mountains, shores and dales.

Christopher Shaw

WINDFARM

Eyeless gargantuans rearing up over the horizon
Straddled upon the mountain ridge, with frightening terror.
Arms relentlessly thrashing, slicing the air in endless motion.
Daunting, destructive destroyers.

Roaring breaths, killing the silences, smiting the ears.
Slayers of beauty, souring the sight, crushers of nature.
Rapers of content, pillagers of peace.
Rising to dominate the skyline with harsh presence

Man-made objects that stand grotesquely above the valley.
Unyielding skeletal aggressors intimidating all beneath.
Portents of the past and future horrors in the name of progress.
Harbingers of the apocalypse to come.

Gone the sweet silences on the heights
No more the soaring lark's concerto
The soft fern and bracken bed replaced with concrete
Tranquillity abused, to exist no more

Never to see again the welcoming curves of your form
As refreshing as water to a thirsting throat.
No longer to recognise the hills of home
Made monstrous and deformed by man's own greed.

Anne Whitcombe Sterry

THE MOUSER

Slinking, sliding and striding,
Whiskers rolling and unfolding,
Eyes brightening and widening,
Gaze twitching, bewitching,
Ears pricking, ticking.
Hush now.
Standing motionless for just one moment.

Rush now.
Pouncing, a rustle, a cuffuffle,
A howl, a growl,
Hissing, spitting,
Meow.

The deed is done!

Louisa Diamond

SPIRAL

Like Crusoe you notch each day.
Each day of your ordeal.
Arm held out, stiff as wood,
While you make your notch.

Deeper and more vivid with every day,
The cut is essential,
So you know where you are.
Like Hansel and Gretel,

You can trace your way to the start.
Without your marks, your control
Is gone. You cry, because you're lost.
Lost and spinning out of control

like a leaf in the wind
round and round and round
until you feel dizzy and sick
helpless until you mark

your position and red springs
burst forth telling you you're
alive and in danger.
Danger of collapse.

So, you make your notch,
To keep control.

Andrew Archibald

HEARTBREAK AND HOPE

She sat alone and wondered
As she trembled in her chair
How her life had come to this
Full of anguish and despair.

Her children were asleep now
Of this fact she was glad
She couldn't bear to see them
So nervous and so sad.

She pondered about leaving
But she had nowhere to go
She couldn't leave her children
Because she loved them so.

The clock upon the wall
Was ticking loud and clear
She knew that her tormentor
Would very soon be here.

Then all at once the silence
Was broken by the sound
Of the gate squeaking open
And him stumble to the ground.

He staggered up the pathway
He banged upon the door
She opened it, and forced a smile
Then looked down to the floor.

He said that he was leaving
He said it was too late
Too late to reconcile their love
That all he felt was hate.

She felt her heart sink to the floor
After all, she was his wife
But then she remembered
Her sad and anguished life.

She felt relief as well as pain
As he left and went away
But she wouldn't have to fear again
Or tolerate his way.

Carol Lewis

AUTUMN WONDER

To walk along a lonely country lane
To see the bright blue sky with puffs of cloud

To scent the chilly tang of crisp cool air
To feel it in my nostrils' flaring shock

To watch the twist and turn of spiralling leaves
Form a golden crunchy carpet underfoot

Observe the hedgerows glisten with morning dew
That falls like melting raindrops to the ground

To feel the fernfronds bending in the breeze
Stretching the spiders' webs like silky nets

To wonder at the colour changes of the leaves
And the berries' red abundance in the trees

Listen to the magpies' chatter as they argue
About the kestrel that hovers high above

Watch the squirrels leap from branch to branch
As busily they store their winter food

In the meadows see the cattle as they
Munch the luscious sweetness' last green grass

All these are things of pleasure that we enjoy
God's wonderful creation - putting earth to rest.

G Gunter

THE WITCHES' CAVE

The overgrown cave stood amidst the tangle,
Shrubs and thorns lay scattered there.
I peered through the entrance curious of
      what I would find.
And straight ahead of me I saw a group of witches,
Bending over a bubbling pot.
The atmosphere seemed so unreal.
My instinct was to run away from this
What seemed unearthly doom like place,
But instead my pride pushed me on.
I neared them feeling uneasy of what would happen,
      should they discover me.
On the ledges stood jars of all shapes and sizes.
Labelled of the species which they held inside.
Then one hunchbacked witch turned around, the
      others following her gaze as she did.
Their faces were old and haggard.
Their hair in streaks from underneath their tall
      pointy hats.
Their hands were wrinkled as they popped
ingredients into the pot, which made me shudder.
A frog's eye, snake's poison, spider's cobweb,
      rat's tail.
They started to chant, faster and faster each
      time.
They had not seen me, luckily enough thought I,
I took one last look around that doom looking
      cave.
For I could not breathe,
The smell was intolerable.
Then I ran outside, not wanting ever to return
      to this uncanny place again.

Amanda Iles

HATRED

Is life that bad you have to kill
do you do it for kicks
or just the thrill
carry on and read what I have to say
because, it could be your life one day.

Stop don't take his life
throw down the gun put down that knife
think about what you are doin'
it's not just his life but your own you ruin.
You may be full of anger and hate
but think,
is he someone's dad or someone's mate,
so before you decide to take a life
Think
because the next time,
it could be you, your mother, father,
child or maybe your wife . . .

Dariann S

MY LAND

Bloodied faces, muddied hands
Cheering men in rugby stands.
Happy people laughing loud
Talking fast and walking proud.
Streets all wet with summer rain
Steaming valleys - dry again.
Mighty mountains green and brown
Straining up and sweeping down.
Streams that shimmer in the sun
'Look at us, how smooth we run,
How lucky can a person be?
This perfect Wales belongs to me!

Yvonne Lewis

SUMMER

Surely the loveliest months of them all,
Are the months of summer, before the fall.
They follow the spring, who gave colour and life,
To an earth that lay still after winter's cruel ice,
They dazzle and thrill us, with a beauty sublime,
These months we call summer, this wonderful time.
Golden warm beaches, and sparkling clear waves,
We get warm, then we cool off, in damp shady caves.
Luscious green fields and heather clad hills,
Waterwheels turning by crumbling old mills.
Village greens that echo to the sound of sport,
Granddad in his deckchair sipping his port.
Warm balmy evenings for young lovers to stroll,
In a world of their own, which is always their role.
Oh if only it could always be summer like this,
But she fades, and she leaves us, without even a kiss.

V Hurford

MY STREET

A small cul-de-sac with ten semis
With ten gardens all in a row.
When the flowers all bloom in the summer
Their colours are a wonderful show.

The neighbours are all very friendly
As I pass there's a pleasant 'Hello'
With a smile that warms up a wintry day
As along with my business I go.

I live in a wonderful area
Where the people are caring and sweet.
And I thank my Father in Heaven
For my home in such a pleasant little street.

Elizabeth Hughes

UNREQUITED LOVE

Heart ruling head,
Knowing he doesn't care,
persevering anyway,
No luck,
No love in return,
Only rejection.
Rejection hurts.
Then again so does love they say.
Yet I know.

I love him, he loves me,
A simple equation
But not true.
It's unbalanced now.
I love him, he doesn't love me.
No chemistry between us.

Rhian Prosser

JIGSAW

Life is like a jigsaw, putting pieces together,
Every piece separate, but needing each other.
Bright colours. Sombre hues, light and shade,
From this confusion a picture is made.

Start out slowly move things around,
Testing and trusting is this solid ground?
People we meet, places we travel,
Parts of the jigsaw we hope to unravel.

The pattern is hard, the picture unclear,
We keep adding to it our joy and our fear.
Peaceful clear water, trouble and strife,
The picture is whole it's the jigsaw of life.

Barbara Hulse

WHERE THE ARTIST LIVES

Here, past busy-lizzie climbing the wall
And more plants in the hall
The artist lives.
It's an absolute clutter!
At a first glance.
There is paper, pots, pens and old scrawls
That the artist hoards.
Splodges of paint, brushes and paste
That the artist scatters all over the place.
Yet! After a chance to search the walls
Here is an Aladdin's cave!
Which the artist created with pleasure.
Signs of life's images capturing time
Portraying what was seen when the artist climbed
To another place, where beauty and calm caught the eye.
Each fleeting moment was captured and held
In a deep mood and tone.
Here, in a world on his own
Is where the artist lives.

Kath Wood

CHILDREN OF WAR

Innocent children playing in the street,
not knowing of the fate they are going to meet
the laughter stops the smiles turn to fear,
as the bombs and gunshot both draw near.

They run for cover and try to survive,
hoping their families they can find alive
childhood is supposed to be smiles and fun,
not hiding from a stranger aiming a gun.

Children bleeding and crying in pain,
best friend lying next to him others slain
children missing death is all around,
innocent little bodies lying on the ground.

But these little kids they have learnt the score,
Stop killing the innocent don't hurt them anymore
Everyday more pain and somebody else dies
and all the children of war hear
are the screams and the cries.

Carolyn McLeod

DARK NIGHTS OF THE SOUL

Adrift, and aimless, meandering in the dark,
Call out! And searching for a mark,
Tumbling into the valley's night,
Lost, and misted out of sight.

Long and desolate these dark nights,
No hand to rescue, to remove the frights,
Swimming in a black abyss,
Lift me please, out of this.

Then the climb to a mortal peak,
Striving, upward, the top to seek,
To another plateau to start again,
Then drop, and ascend, just the same.

Till in the end we reach the one,
That is the top, we can now succumb,
For the last dark night has come to pass,
Our souls have found their glory, never to surpass.

George Colley

THE SUNDAY GAME

The boots are laced,
the shin pads in place,
determination is etched on his face.
The shirt is tucked in,
the shorts on the hips,
needles and thread have erased the past rips.

He takes up his position
on the damp, green grass,
mentally visualising the ideal pass.
His opponent is greeted
with eyebrows raised,
a nod of the head and indifferent gaze.

'Good luck to you both
and give it your best!'
The man in black puffs out his chest
and blows on the whistle.
An invisible shield
protects him from the melee on the field.

'Man on!' 'Oi, mate!'
'Are you blind, referee?'
'Over here!' 'Sort the wall!' 'Our striker's free!'
'Keep the ball down!'
'My ball!' 'Shoot!'
'It's wide!' 'How'd he miss?' 'Give him the boot!'

Tensions are high.
Tempers are short.
Precious points are being sought
by men who are friends
when off the field -
but enemies true with studs to wield.

The final whistle
puts an end
to tackles too desperate to comprehend.
The scores are level -
both teams fare the same
and agree, shaking hands, that it's only a game.

Julie A Kinnair

LET NATIONS HEED A DREAMER'S CALL

Let nations of the world unite
To bring a future pure and bright
Let war be taken far away
Bring peace forever here to stay
Let violent men be treated such
And those of peace admired as much
As much as angels as they are
Give help to heal what violence scarred
Let nature's heart be soothed by all
What wonders of the world she calls
Let the beauty of her voice be heard
Let nations hear her every word
Let choking skies be cleared like new
The murky turned to purest blue
Let nations of the world unite
Through troubled times all join and fight
Join and fight to ease the pain
Take tragic times bring love again
Let grievances be buried deep
Let children young all peaceful sleep
Now let me sleep and wake again
Today tomorrow but only when
When nations of the world unite
And bring a future pure and bright

Gareth Lovell

SILENCE OF THE LAMB

Panorama of pleasure the vista of life
Who studies the forests or ponders their strife
In footpaths of virtues and pastures of sin
Adonis, Narcissus sleep sheltered within

Our chronicled sojourn through passage of time
Instinctive desires considered a crime
Intrinsic prison for impious thought
Inflamed by raw passion - morality bought

We tether our freedom build intangible walls
Repress our emotions subdue nature's call
Sow social acceptance from infertile seed
Our bounteous harvest crops pernicious weed

May we drink our desire flaunt naked intent
Follow our star map its course or ascent
Through bud burst and blossom leaf fall to last fruit
Needs lamentably tailored from societies' suit

Dare we liberate spirit and liberate mind
Discover the treasure that fetters mankind
That fleck of perception the soupçon that steeps
Infuse our whole being recumbent asleep.

Lynden Tanner

WALES

Oh Wales you land of glorious song;
It's where my heart with you belongs.
Your lovely towns and valleys green.
There is nowhere else such beauty seen.

Bore da to you, our kith and kin;
God bless you all who live within
This land of love and of great tales.
There is no better place than Wales.

From the Rhondda valley great men came
And gave to the world this place called Wales,
As love and song were their delight
With that lovely song 'All Through The Night'.

Where the names of Davies and of Jones
Who have this land to call their home,
Whether over land or sea they sail,
Their names forever will stay in Wales.

Francis Allen

DELIRIUM (FOR SELWYN)

Some say
The wind carries the
Unfulfilled hopes
Of generations,
And screams for them
In mourning.
For the bitterness
And sorrow
Of hopes snatched away
From them, and
Blown to oblivion
By a cruel
Intoxicating,
Powerful force
Which cannot be seen
Or explained.
Yet,
Envelops, destructs,
Without intention,
And seeks
Unacknowledged forgiveness
By setting itself
In warp.

Rhiannon Hart

SWIMMING

Splashing and swimming
Lengths and widths,

Diving under and
Doing the splits.

Under the water
Squiggle and squirm,

Swimming is lots of
fun to learn.

Under the ocean
Under the sea,

Swimming under
Swimming free.

The End

Stephanie Connors

GOD'S IMAGE

The suns are like the eyes of man, the winds and rains like souls,
The oceans in the bloodstream flows, God's image is the role.
Humanity's the thought of God, the plants express the lung,
All life portrays emotions and has done since time begun.

The soil is as man's bowels and is where our roots are based,
It's here and now our learning starts and living's to be faced.

How can we say we're lonely and cry in anguished pain,
When all we have to do is look and see we're all the same.

If we could only stop and grasp what Christ had come to show,
We'd know that he's been all these things and we must try to follow.

Frances Wright

PIT CLOSURE

They closed another pit today
and laid off all the men.
Just a handful left to salvage
but most won't work again.
No more to toil in darkness
crouched up in three foot seams.
To scratch an honest living
to fulfil their hopes and dreams.

The multi-million pound machines
stand idly in the dust.
Gigantic metal monsters
just left behind to rust.
Their wheels bogged down
in muck and coal,
their future too is cast.
They'll lay beneath the
earth's dark crust,
a relic of the past.

Unlike the men who tunnelled
in the bowels of the earth.
Who'd struggle on regardless
for far less than their worth.
Their lamps still burning brightly
but with little breath to spare.
Still yearning for the blackness,
beneath the earth somewhere.

Catherine Mary Millard

WAR

Screaming and crying,
Many people dying,
Soldiers stamped,
Everybody's cramped.

Soldiers don't care,
Lots of people stare,
Countries torn apart,
Does anyone have a heart?

I don't think I really want to see the world this way,
I would rather like to see the little children play.
I just can't wait for the day
When I hear the news say,
All the wars are over,
Little children go and play.

Rebecca Hurle (13)

WHITE SATIN

In white satin she did lie.
When her time had come to die.
Beautiful was the face she showed.
Before the lid was gently closed.

Family, neighbours and good friends.
Say goodbye with the flowers they send.
But in their hearts they soon discover.
It takes time to recover.

The mother, lover and the sister.
No matter who, all will miss her.
The pain and grief will ease in time.
But she will live forever in their mind.

Joan Sayers

MICHAEL

His mind was not as quick as yours or mine.
His eyes, not quite in focus, skimmed the surface of the page,
Seeing patterns that made no sense.
Numbers, letters, what?
His body, clumsy, slight and dirty,
Not in any way appealing,
Smelled.
His conversation, vague, described a violent video,
Watched at 2 am.
Thoughts of food suddenly filled his mind,
And animal instinct sent him running, roaring,
Towards the bell.
Eleven years of hunger, cold and neglect,
Have made him a survivor.
What else has life to offer this little scrap?

Anne Savan

BYGONE DAYS

Gone the days when a child could play both far and near
And mother knew she had nought to fear

Respect for teachers and elders is what we had
A telling off from the police if we were bad

Not having to make your home like a jail
Or being attacked when you're old and frail

Walking the streets without a feeling of dread
And knowing you were safe when you went to bed

Oh to have those days once more
When you did not have to lock your door

M L Cartwright

A SOLDIER'S FAREWELL

From El Alemein to Lombardy a soldier had to fight.
Battle after battle, he fought with main and might
From scorching African desert sand, to northern plains of Italy,
Onwards! Onwards! Ever onwards! Pursuing his adversary.
There at last across the plains, as far as mortal eyes could see,
Preparing for a final stand, the proud and mighty enemy.
No more to yield one inch of ground, by God! They'd fight and die,
E'en though their final resting place was not beneath their homeland sky.
To and fro the battle raged with much ferocity,
For to the victor go the spoils of war,
On the 'Bloody Plains' of Lombardy.
Above the battle's din, I heard a soldier pray.
'My Lord! My Lord! My dearest Lord! Give me strength,
Show me the way, that in this hour of victory,
I will with true humility, not give way to hating;
But forgive my enemy, as you did in the past,
On your cross at Calvary.'
Once more brave comrades, let's to the fray.
'Twas the Colonel's last command,
For now he lay a-dying, in this 'Bloody Foreign Land'.
At last we breached the enemy lines, and one by one their heroes fell,
Until no enemy soldier did this day live to tell.
Alas! In this our finest hour of glorious victory,
I searched in vain for the one who prayed, but his face I could not see,
And I knew my valiant comrade - though only twenty summers liveth he -
Had found his final resting place on 'The Bloody Plains' of Lombardy.

Henry Ward

THE SOUTH WESTERN WIND

Oh how I hate you, the one from south west
The mighty, devilish without no rest
Perfidious, cold and penetrating
Terrible, strong and unrepenting.

The wind of winds who blows our way
Without the mercy, without dismay
Chill our bones, soul and flesh
You never stop but start afresh.

When you blow so merciless no heart
No senses are safe, body apart
Killing the flesh, numb our feet
I hate you mighty south western wind.

K Gmur

SOUL MATE

My heart it aches
My soul it quakes
My thoughts abound
They chase me
Like a hound!

What is this thing?
That treats me so
It takes me where
I don't want to go!

My love for you
It is so deep
I give it now
For you to keep!

E Bevan

ELIN MAIR

Like a fair young sapling, she moves around.
Hair blowing freely, sometimes not a sound.
Then all at once, with arms flying wild,
She hurls herself at me, my grandchild.
Her eyes so intense and agog with life
Fighting with me, as Robin Hood's wife.
Then dying the sleep of the fair aurora,
And coming back to me in a dreamy amourer.
Who cares about World Cup trauma?
When heaven is curled up beside you
And the sound of her breathing is warmer
Than any World Cup trauma.
She likes my beads and ear-rings too
And says so quietly, 'I love you.'
On leaving her, when it's time to go,
'Will you come back, Granny-Ma?
I love you so.'

V Markham

ROAD BUILDING

Sometimes I think we've all gone mad
We've more roads now than we ever had
And still they want to build lots more
So we can ride from door to door
The loss of canal, buses and train
Seems green field's loss is concrete's gain
We can't replace the fields and trees
When there's not homes left for the birds and bees
It's time we came to our senses
We cannot afford all these expenses.

M M Watts

DRUNKEN VENUS

Hide in the white apple trees
With the drunken Venus, watch as
She rages for throats and eyes
With broken bottles, nails, marble, flowers . . .

Your friend's lover. She hates you.
Watch as the slivers of glass
Sing past your ears, as she
Pushes you into roads, into cars . . .

Then watch with your ruffled hair
As she pauses her drunken storms,
Watch as she strokes your face
With a smiling and ineffable calm.

Kristian Evans

WOODLANDS GREEN

I love to walk through woodlands green
And see flowers in abundance
All colours with fragrance to be seen
The sun peeps through hedges different coloured leaves
My dog wags his tail happiness seems to be on his face
As I walk through this beautiful place
Time to me has no meaning when I walk upon this ground
I stop and listen to the birds
Singing and chicks tweeting in nests
All is quiet only their sound
I see butterflies and bumble bees
Sucking nectar from the flowers
And I see tall trees reaching to the sky
All this done by God's almighty hand
Across this earth and this dear land.

Arnold R Williams

THE LOVERS

The stars shine down on a land that is still
The breeze whispers softly, a crisp autumn chill
Beauty encased in a black velvet shroud
Nothing can be heard but the softest of sounds
Of two hearts beating softly, eyes shining bright
Hidden away neath the veil of night
In darkness entwined, their bodies as one
Twisting and turning, illicit with fun
Turning hours to minutes, time flits away
The Lovers unnoticed are discovered by day
As the sun rises slowly, the birds cease their calm
The Lovers entwined in each other's arms
Covered in moisture, the dawn's early dew
Speckles of diamonds, glistening hues
Of silvers and yellows, of greens and of browns
Clothing the Lovers with Nature's fresh gowns
Until they awake in the cold chill of morn
Sleepy yet vibrant for they are reborn
In love that is precious, love that is pure
Love that is timeless in heady allure
They go on their way in the cool morning light
Completely refreshed by the passions of night.

Mark Dorey

OVER THE RAINBOW

Over the rainbow, tiny angels rest,
Upon the purest whitest silk.
Surrounded by the softest petals
Amidst the sweetest scent.
Over the rainbow, a heavenly glow
Caresses a star of magical silver,
And a halo of peace shines down.

Rebecca Punter

FEELINGS WITHIN

Express feelings in your mind
Then put them into action.
Tell the people that you care
And feel the satisfaction.
Uncomfortable as it is
They're better out than in.
People cannot guess
What you feel within.

No rules for what you're feeling
No chapter to act out
Confusing that it is on times
Your feelings will come out.
No guide to life and living,
No right way to get by.
Just follow what you're feeling
Your mind it must not shy.

Honesty within comes first
Before you open up.
Be at peace with your own mind
You'll quietly raise up.
No one will be wiser
About your inner thoughts.
But satisfaction you will feel
A lesson has been taught.

Julie Jones

THE PRICE OF COAL - NO 2

Turn back the page of time
You'll see men killed and maimed in their prime.
Working long hours without a rest
So the coal lords can feather their nests.
While miners' families scrape and strive
Just to keep body and soul alive.
Children and young girls worked down that hole
That my friends was the price of coal.

The disasters that occurred down through the age
Fill all miners' hearts with terrible rage.
The horror of sliding slag tips
Still brings a tremble to so many lips.
The coughing of a dust filled chest
Men dead, long before they are laid to rest.
And it seems that their only role
Is to pay the terrible price of coal.
Now turn to the present age
Miners striking for a living wage.
They not only ruin their health in the mine
But have to fight for their rights all along the line.
Surely they deserve a much better deal
Who will pay not the owners I feel
Their pockets are too near their soul
So what will go up is the price of coal.

J A Edwards

TO A WELSH SHEEP DOG

The sun it was shining, Di woke with the dawn,
There were cows to be milked on this bright summer morn,
He hurriedly dressed and went for the help,
Of his old faithful sheepdog with the loveable yelp.
'Come on old girl, you are eager to go.'
She trotted beside him, but Di seemed so slow.
The cows were her work, and she scampered ahead,
Then expertly guided them into the shed.
Outside she sat waiting till milking was done,
Then guided them back into the sun.
Di sat on a stone, his pipe for to fill,
While the beauty around them was peaceful and still.

Bess had stayed with her Master for ten years or more,
This loveable sheep dog Di learnt to adore.
Amongst the Welsh hills this faithful old friend
They grew old together right to the end.
The sun it was shining Di woke with the day,
And went to get Bess asleep on the hay.

There was no friendly greeting her duty to keep,
She lay on the hay as if fast asleep.
No breath in her body, no shine in her eye,
Di couldn't believe that she had to die,
Out in the field he bore her away,
Beneath the soft turf he put her to lay.

Di will be lonely without his dear friend,
But when the day comes for his journey's end,
Bess will be waiting to greet him that day.
Down the pathway of Heaven she'll once more lead the way.

Vera Parsonage

THE SUMMER OF '41

'Have you seen it, it's amazing,'
Dicky Lewis said.
'No, I haven't,' whispered me,
Lifting up my head.

'It's exactly like the picture
In the book that Teacher got,
The book that was our favourite
We looked at quite a lot.'

'Is it true,' said Mary Jones,
'It came across the sea?'
'Of course it did in a great big ship,'
Said know-all Billy Lee.

'They say a soldier brought it home.'
'Yes, my uncle,' shouted Lenny,
'And Teacher's rafflin' it today.
The tickets are a penny.'

'It's pink number five,' called Mrs Smith,
'It's me,' screamed snooty Lana,
And off she walked that summer's day
With the prize - a ripe banana.

Jean Davies

GWENT

I went to Gwent,
and the time I spent,
was most enjoyable,
to an extent.

It was very cold,
the frost was down,
there were hills everywhere,
and mountains all around.

The locals were friendly,
they spoke like a song,
their words seemed to rhyme,
no matter how long.

I liked it in Gwent,
tucked away there in Wales,
I will soon come again,
even with their force gales.

R Miles

WAITING

I'm pregnant.
That's all I ever think about.
Other people hate the idea,
other people run a mile away.
Me, I run but towards you.
Nappies, crying, sleepless nights,
give me all and more,
I don't hate or loath.
All I want is to love you and be there for you.
Abortion, adoption,
it's right for some.
But give me a chance that's all.
I want you with all of me,
all my heart, soul and more,
all that I can give, I give to you,
you and my family.
To be a family means more to me
than anything living or dead.
I feel that my whole life has been one pregnancy,
waiting for this moment,
waiting for the moment when I can say,
'Congrats I'm a mum'
Mother!

T E Jeffery

A-MOOSING - COW'S EYE VIEW (*BOVINE SEES EVERYTHING*)

I gaze at the *moo*n but I don't feel mad, but Buttercup vanished today
He dug a hole at the dead of night, and her manure on the vegetables sprayed.

He's mumbling about Europe who don't want our beef
As he picks his bits of Daisy out of his teeth
He wants his grants to pay back the bank
He writhes in distress with his mind all blank.

His children are playing they don't look mad
If they're naughty he looks a little sad
I've heard we will burn in heaps in the night
But if they've got CJD it must be a fright.

If I hadn't eaten sheep's brains in my pellets
The price of death, well, I'd not have to pay it
He hopes he can feed us and still sell out milk
Then get paid out by Europe - his pocket of silk.

I feel like spinning, I'm loony, the moon full does shine
I fancy a hedgehog as my valentine.
My legs are like jelly made out of old bones
My relative's inheritance: gelatine rot and mad moans.

Can't he see it's too late they've all eaten mad cows
Drunk all the milk, spread butter so now
If they kill us our calves will still carry disease
A brilliant government likes death, save money please.

At least ministers will die with the rest
They were mad at the start, don't care, made this mess.
People go batty and cows they will burn
But BSE in the land is here long, long term.

The hedgehog has gone it prefers scrapie sheep
The moon now is waning, it's dark I can sleep
I look at the pigs, the chicks and the ducks
All fed on the mess - the country is mucked!

Shelley Southwood-Clarke

MY VALLEY, THE CYNON

The valleys of Wales are many,
Each boasting out the Welsh splendour.
There's the Merthyr and Rhondda both stunning,
And the Rhymney as lovely as ever.
Now another you have to remember,
The greatest one of all,
It is of course, the one we love most, the Cynon standing up tall.
My valley, the Cynon, how are you today?
All dressed up in your colours of May.
I do like that bonnet you wear with such pride,
All covered with rivers and mountains abide.
Oh look at that lamb so innocent and mild,
You're ever so lucky to have such a child.
And what of your famous grey rainclouds today?
I didn't think that they'd ever go away.
But now we can see how exquisite you can be,
It would be nice to see this up till January.
I will miss your spring flowers that do captivate,
I suppose they too have to hibernate.
Your coalmines are famous for miles around,
How grateful you are to those men underground.
Through winter crisp snow lays thick on your skin,
Now is the time the snow-sports begin.
Through autumn your colours dazzle us all,
When all your leaves do curl up and fall.
Oh Cynon we thank you all year around,
Where in your valley all happiness is found.
My valley, the Cynon how we all love you so,
I hope I never see the day when you have to go.

Gareth Hughes

POBLADO HEIGHTS

Crickets chirp busily, frogs compete.
Moths flit by on wings of light.
The moon
encased in a mist of eerie shadows,
The song of night birds, shrill, pervades the night.
Shrubs are frozen in electric radiance.
Street lights glow as from unseen post.
A car moves slowly,
Its lights sweeping the empty streets
as if searching for the anticipated welcome.
The beams pass smoothly, silently over homes
Outlined and friendly,
Like silent faces promising refuge.
The cool night air prickles the senses
Night flowers' fragrant perfume
intoxicates, a tease.
And in the distance
Far away and into the night
The mountains hover
Their presence felt.
Outlined yet vague, in silent mood.

A D Jones

A CRY TO THE SINGING WIND

I, love the green fields and the cry of the plover,
The wind on my face whispering 'Winter's now over'
The view of my home from a lone mountain track,
The sun warm and strong beating down on my back.
My feet feeling firm on the green hillside turf.
This is my heaven, down here, on this earth.
These things I love, with a love that enthralls me -
O'er all these things is my love - and trust in thee.

Hubert John Evans

FERGUS

A tiny tiger stalking through the grass
Tip toes fastidiously on dainty paws.
He shakes the dewdrops in a showery mass
Which splash like tears on prehensile claws.

His stripes are painted by a master's hand;
Their shades are vying for ascendancy.
Around his tail each darker, tawny band
Encircles it with measured artistry.

At night two beacons will appear - his eyes
Which glow like topaz jewels polished bright.
They flash their fiery sparks to mesmerise
All living creatures with their golden light.

And if he deigns to let you hold him close,
His body trembles with each rhythmic purr.
Life gushes through him with dynamic force,
Vibrating in his coat of silky fur.

Coiled like a spring, in action swift and sure,
Pheidippides could never run like this.
With rippling muscles taut he will endure
The longest marathon with nought amiss.

And when he rests, oblivion will enfold
This gentle kitten in its opiate sleep.
Lost to the world, his busy life on hold,
Until he wakes, his sculptured form he'll keep.

Celia G Thomas

TRUE LOVE WAITS

A glance bestowed and I'm complacent,
If you are despondent I am melancholic.
A touch from your hand shivers my spine
And the scent of you is unforgettable.
Your deep alluring orb shows me in reflect, yet -
You are hesitant while I am resolute in my
enamoured infatuation.

In the clutches of love you are enigmatic,
I look at you,
You look away.
Am I so perceptible you glow?
I am replete with you, while you magnify on my
zealous embryonic being,
And out of this dreamy love,
I am forgetful of whom I am.

Yet if in the clutches of love why is my heart wrenched?
The resounding, caustic momentum,
Beating in time for a faltering feeling.
My juvenescence, psalm, and endeavouring assault
leave you negligent.
I become an empty vessel, long awaiting love,
Long awaiting you.

Kelly Davies (17)

MOTHER'S HEARTACHE

I did not need to hear her cries
I only had to look into her eyes.

She was in a state of shock,
His heart must be made of rock.

How could he cause her so much pain?
Now she'll never be the same.

When he left, it broke her heart,
Her whole world just fell apart.

Now life continues for my mother,
But can she learn to trust another?

Michelle Hughes

THE MOUNTAIN WALL

I walked beside a mountain wall
So grey with age and lichens small.
That did from craggy summit leap
To meadow fair and waters deep.

Beside it, lofty foxgloves grow
Its shelter pale primroses know.
Bramble and bracken, gorse and heather
Mingle profusely there together.

On boundary line twixt field and wood
A guardian sentinel it stood.
That neither harboured trespass fears
But peaceful dwelt through passing years.

Mountain sheep huddling close keep warm
While the hillsides swept by the wild snowstorm.
Scared rabbits within its crevices hide
When wily fox stalks his prey alongside.

Rough its stones nor hewn by hand
As they were gathered from the land.
No mortar binds them in their tiers,
Yet firm they stand throughout the years.

The hands that built it now are dust
The tools they wielded turned to rust.
But to those skilful toilworn hands
A monument today it stands.

R E Harper

HOPE

You make me feel just like a child!
An angelic voice that sings inside
My soul, that feels so empty with no air,
A breeze which whispers bleak despair.

You are a vision in my sight,
So understanding of my plight.
The struggle that twists blade-like in sleep,
And bleeds at day from wounds so deep.

I wish, I dream of better things,
Of nightingales with coloured wings
Who fly so freely, unaware
Of how they destroy my bleak despair.

I pick my orchid, deep red tones,
Their fragrance ebbs away my moans.
I smell the flower fixed in my gaze,
Now I know how to spend my days.

In places where there's only joy,
Where I am not played like any toy.
Where love is free and given with ease
Like crystal waves on azure seas.

Two-fold meanings disappear,
Freedom, reigns within my ear.
What of these lines, how do they seem?
Are they mere images of a dream?

Simon D Ford

RHYTHM CHASER

Rhythm chaser
Master of rhyme
Bringer of passion
The loveable swine.

Pulling the heart strings
Of gullible girls.
Creating a poem
With elegant twirls.

Many may be jealous
Of his poetic powers.
But to think of a rhyme
Must take him hours.

The god of all words,
The speaker of truth.
The singer of love
The dictionary sleuth.

Immortal in rhyme
A verse for all time.
Flow from the tongue
Of an improvised line.

Chasing the rhythm
Mastering the rhyme.
Casting the spell
Immortal in time.

Richard Lewis Cooke

THEY

They talk at you, but never to you
Syrup of fig coated jargonese,
Balloons from their cardboard mouths
With the same laxative affect.
They hear you, but they don't listen.
You are a small disposal cog
In their five year corporate business plan.
There to assuage the hunger pangs
Of the new technology that dominates the workplace,
To feed the cavernous bellies,
Of the bulimic machines.
That spew out ream upon ream of paper
Until the rainforests weep.
They are the new employers in this take over world.

P H Hunt

FA CUP FINAL 1996

Twin Towers stadium here we come
The kop, no doubt, will be on the run.
Sea of red spells Manchester Utd,
Tears of excitement shed.
Ferguson, Kidd, point the way
Cantona will dominate they pray.
Supportive moves from Keane and May,
Giggs gallops down the wing.
United now in full swing,
Liverpool attempts punched from sight.
This happens to be Schmeichel plight.
Sharp odds on to score a goal and hopefully Cole
Seal a win that's all United know.
Red Army soldiers on home
Claiming the champions' throne.

Alan Jones

CASTLE

The cold exterior
So rough and raw.
Hideously silhouettes itself
Against the backdrop of a surreal sky.
It imposes its form
On the landscape of life,

Claiming the importance it has to play.
How blind is this sky and this land?
Which shun the very battlements
Discrediting their worth.
How insensitive and superficial are these beauties?

These outward fineries,
Which inevitably fade with time.
Yes, it has watched
As many serene skies lose their brilliance.
Observed how countless winters
Have ravished and overcome
Marring that handsome landscape which surround it.

They fail to notice,
The extensive charm of this great building
Whose beauty lies within.
If they but demeaned themselves to take a glance,
For inside the severe fortress,
Is hidden an inner grace of character,
Which never dies so long as the structure stands.

This internal glow grows, rather than decays,
And would be welcoming to visitors,
If they took time to examine the depth of interior glory,
Which is too easily overlooked.

Jane Collins

DARKNESS

Angel of darkness, conviction of fear,
Shadows and trees where demons appear.
Darkness is black, hooded and blind,
Deep fearful thoughts chastising the mind.

Mad dogs and drunks, disturbance of calm,
Sleepy young children, innocence and charm.
Streets quiet and calm without hustle or bustle,
Wild cat and mouse fighting angry mad tussle.

Nightmares and dreams in full colourvision
New babies cry and mother's arisen.
Badgers and foxes out hunting their prey,
Nocturnal creatures frightened by day

Sun in the sky, birds in the trees,
Fresh morning dew, coolness of breeze.
Eggs, bread and milk breakfast is here,
Male heads pounding from glasses of beer.

Commuters and trains, daily routine,
No more thoughts for the night laden with dream.
Day passes by embracing nightfall,
So it's back to our beds shadows and all.

Mark Jones

GOD'S GOOD LAND

Why are we spoiling our countryside
    and why are we ruining the land?
Why are we destroying all that is good
    created by God's dear hands.

Why do we cut the trees down
    in rainforests, where beautiful birds once lived.
Don't we care at all, how much is destroyed?
    All the wonders, the Good Lord gives.

It's now time for the world to listen
        before it is left too late.
Let us not destroy our beautiful world
        as we're doing, at a very fast rate.

Think not of ourselves, but of our God and King
        and help to care for His world, for Him
For the Lord put all nature in our hands
        so let's not destroy God's good land.

J A Parry

THE STREET I LOVED

In the Rhondda
In Bygone days.
Was a little street
Where I was raised
Called Fernhill Houses.
Up on a hill.
The memories are with me sill.

Although the street isn't there anymore,
Sometimes back to the place I go.
I love to sit there
And think of the past
Of Fernhill Houses
The memories still last.

I imagine the people I used to know
And the children I played with so long ago.
A better street was never found
I'm standing on enchanted ground.

Christine Williams

INCOMPLETE HEAVEN

I stand apart,
my senses filled with exaltation.
The pleasant breeze gently caresses my hair,
a kind respite from the fiery heat of the sun.
I breathe deep, inhaling stainless air
simple joy.

Wilfully, the sea shatters against the leaden rocks below,
churning the spreading water into white cream.
Spraying freshness as the soothing rhythm of its
order resounding breaks the silence.
I shade my eyes and look beyond at the turquoise water
which is sprinkled silver by the sun.

Joy fills my heart
I have learnt to find happiness in my perpetual dwelling place.
Vigilant to nature's intensity,
I float in liberation.
Yet I know my heaven is incomplete,
A fundamental part of me is still missing.

The seasons change, but my longing does not cease,
In paradise loneliness still has no actual ending.
True love can have no cure,
I take pleasure from my spirit sphere.
But my thoughts I exclude for heedfulness
of my aching core.

A chapel wall extends its welcome,
its whiteness reflects the sun.
I sit in the coolness of its embrace,
I feel sorrow, alone within my heaven,
and wait with a yearning heart for my faithful love to join my
scattered ashes.

Moira Lloyd

FORGOTTEN RHONDDA

Memories of a forgotten past,
When pride and coal were together cast.
Bygone days of coal and dust,
Now the colliery wheel has turned to rust.
So to Rhondda Heritage Park we flock,
To see the legacy of that black rock.
With Tommy-box and Billy-can,
Where are you now my collier man?

Still let's not immortalise the past,
Remember Aberfan? The Cambrian blast.
For those were days of want and toil,
But the community it didn't spoil.

The churches once stood straight and proud,
With honour our fore-fathers had endowed.
Monoliths of an age gone by
Religion no longer held on high.

From leek and daffodil high on a hill,
To worrying about the council tax bill.
'Amateur dramatics!' - For those who care,
The new found theme of the Parc and Dare.
Pubs and clubs still spew forth their ale,
Well they know this weary tale.
To pride and place at the Arms Park,
Where men of scarlet make their mark.
Gareth Edwards, Barry John,
Where have all my heroes gone?

So from Penrhys to the valley floor,
From the dole queues to the factory door.
Say a prayer for my Rhondda man,
And sing me one more Calon Lan.

C Evans

I CLOSE MY EYES

I close my eyes and see the valley as it once was,
The mountains guarding the houses on its slopes.
The stream gurgles on its way past the church,
Engines pulling trucks to the pithead.
Past the house where I was born,
One of a row together for strength,
This is the Gwent that I loved.

So I hesitate to open my eyes, but it must be so,
The mountains are guarding a change.
The church is standing, but no stream passes,
No engines puff on a non existent line.
No pithead stands, the centre takes its place,
My house is gone, swallowed by a new school.

Who could be indifferent to change,
or think badly of all that is good in Gwent?

W H Baghurst

ODE TO OUR SWEET LOVE (6 YELLOW ROSES)

The first and the second for the years
we've been wed.
The third for the sweet girl we made
in our bed.
The fourth and the fifth for the boys
we both love
The sixth to show the path of our love

The thorns for the hard times we conquer
so well.
The petals so soft like your touch and your smile
The colour of sun which lights up our lives,
I'm lucky to see every day in your eyes.

G R Evans

THE IN-LAWS

The in-laws are special
For without them
I would not have
My sweet little gem.

To Ken and Sylvia
I say a hearty Ta
For the joy they've given
To me from afar.

For love and respect
Is what I feel
For what I have
From when I did kneel.

For without their fruit
Who became my wife
And with whom
I gave new life.

Joy for us all
An angel so fair
Such fun to be with
Blue eyes and blonde hair.

Things do change
It's a fact of life
My feelings won't
Through trouble and strife.

A final word
For you special two
For all I have now
A big 'Thank You.'

Christopher Herdman

GWENT

Here I live in the county of Gwent,
from Llanhilleth to Six Bells I went.
There's lots of places to visit and view,
And plenty of things to occupy you.
Go and enjoy a swim in the baths,
Or go for a walk up the mountain paths.
Shop at Newport, Ebbw Vale or Brynmawr,
Some people are rich here and some are poor.
There's Bryn Bach Park and Tredegar House too,
Unless you'd rather visit a zoo?
And also we have Cwmcarn Scenic Drive,
Go for a picnic when you arrive
In Cwmbran, Greenmeadow Community Farm.
Go to the country where all's quiet and calm,
There's the Big Pit Museum,
Mines there, you can see 'em.
For me Gwent is a nice place to be,
I'd rather live here than near the sea.

K Brown

AN EXILE'S RETURN

When I close my eyes, I'll see forever,
Though my body dies, my soul will never.
Scattered as ashes, or 'moulded in earth',
My spirit will roam its place of birth.

Decades have past and years have gone by,
But the hiraeth of leaving never subsides.
My body in England - my heart in Wales,
My ghost will wander through Rhondda's fair dales.

So weep not for me, only wish me well,
This day should be filled with joy.
Sprinkle my dust from the top of the hill,
Where I once ran as a boy.

Between sweet green grass and eternal blue sky,
It's here I have chosen to lie.
So that I may run with my playmates again,
As soon as I close my eyes.

Denise Jones

WILL YOU WEEP FOR THE CHILDREN?

Will you weep for the children that are hurting so bad? The sick and the hungry, the lonely the sad.
Orphans in countries divided by war, roam the streets aimlessly with feet that are sore.
Who climb over bodies where blood stains the streets, where houses are ruined and bricks lay in heaps
Will you weep for the children who are hungry for bread, who are homeless with nowhere to lay down their head?
Why are their lives being ripped far apart? Why should they have to nurse broken hearts?
Will you weep for the children who are scared and confused? For those who are murdered and awfully abused?
Where is their justice? Who will protect them each day?
Who will make them feel safe and chase their nightmares away?
Will you weep for the children?
Will you be counted and stand?
As one who'll protect them from murderers' hands.

Nigel Power

THE RHONDDA VALUES

Weekly post-pub wars burst randomly,
Almost land-mined streets violently blow
With furious killer intentions and disregard
For actions, outcomes and basic human life.
And curious onlookers become entangled,
In the murderous web of their arm swinging rythmns.
An alcoholics synonymous street ballet,
Seeking bloodthirsty elevations above poverty.

Bill bound giros lost as rapidly as gained,
For the thoughtless, terraced congregations.
Empty, complicated lives of hate and depression,
Or a weekly, sixty-hour wageless snare.
Tightly trapped in family requirements,
And lost among endless lines of production.
This directionless cul-de-sac of employment,
Stifles generations and promotes non-ability.

The mine-lands of past culture lost eternally,
Industrial robotics shape current classes.
But useless yearning only saturates the spirit,
Education encourages the path to cultivation . . .
 - Expose our true civilisation to the masses.
 - Give individual artistic freedom to produce.
 - Find purpose in society's synchronised monotonies.
 - Lead Wales higher than British inferior expectations.

Kai Merriott

METAMORPHOSIS

I watched you today
Your kind, lovely face at play
And fleetingly thought I saw
The sun rise in your expression

Here, in your darkest hour
I saw an inner glow
Newly awoken from sleep
And then my heart
Broke free with yours
As together, we metamorphosise.

Lynda Newington

PERFECTION - A LADY

Your parents had a special gift
To create a lady like you.
As pure as a snowflake
And just as delicate too.

You're as radiant as a rainbow
With all its colours bright.
And many other attributes
That shine like stars at night.

You adorn a beautiful fragrance
A bouquet that fills the air.
Which next to you in all the world
No flower can compare.

You have many precious treasures
Among them, kindness and grace.
And the magic that tells all
The smile upon your face.

You are charming and demure,
Without an ounce of mirth.
You are the very pinnacle
Of perfection here on earth.

Michael Paul Ashcroft

WAR KILLS

Blood and fire, veins of purple
Sirens sound as aircraft hovers.
The evil souls who help to murder,
the peasants and the others.

A time to kill, revenge so savage,
no place to hide or seek.
The uniforms of countries dead,
foul stench of bodies, future bleak.

Dogs devour this time is theirs,
Soldiers weary wait to die.
as they watch with total horror,
houses burn and children cry.

The spoils of war count many victims,
a battle with no identity.
Remember all those friends we lost,
but we survived, you and me.

Suzzanne Westwood

MUSIC OF THE WIND

The music rippled the long growing grass,
Speed deciding how quickly time should pass,
And then it slowed, desiring to pause,
My mind, my body; wanted to recall,

With head reeling I told it to obey,
But the music again carried it away,
I searched for memories for what had just been,
No echoing melody, or repeat of the scene,

The music slowed down to a crawl,
Haunting lines, I endeavoured to recall,
No return this time - someone had decided,
As swirling notes sounded, loud music exploded.

A loud crash, a roar; and the movement ended,
The symphony over, as nature intended,
Silence replaced it, and filled the air,
The orchestra would be playing, to someone, elsewhere.

Peter McNeil

MY SUNSHINE

Shine for me, dance for me,
Brighten my day with your smile.
Stay with me, respectfully
I pray you, just for awhile.
Rise for me, always be
A radiant glow in the sky,
Energy, eternally,
Lifting my spirits up high.
Forever be, close to me,
My trusting, worthy guide.
Never be, far from me
My heart needs all you provide
Follow me, constantly.
Give me the strength you possess,
Reach for me, affectionately
Your power and love I'll invest.
Comfort me, live in me,
Dazzle your golden zest.
Dear to me, free to be
My life and my happiness.

Helen Deborah Bennett

THE SPIRIT OF DARKNESS

I watched the narrowing shaft of light,
As, sinking deeper into the bowels
of the earth the cage closed
around us.
Protecting yet suffocating,
The walls of the deepening tunnel
lengthening, ever deeper
ever faster.
The bottom of the pit
coming to meet us.
Ready to consume and swallow.
Regurgitating, spitting us out
To begin another journey.
Another tunnel another shape, ever darker
Ever longer.
Then silence, only the sound
of scurrying rodents
Disturbed by man.
Light! Coming nearer then disappearing,
gone perhaps many years ago.
Forgetting where it belongs,
Where it should be.
Gone with many others, no longer here.
No longer there, floating, looking
For what should be.
It begins, machinery moaning
drilling into the walls
of black gold.
Dust swirling, clouds thickening
The light searching, still looking,
Through the moonless tunnels of
infinity.

Never resting, never ceasing
always looking
For yesterday.
A yesterday gone that took many.
Their light remains, no longer men
But spirits
And one with the earth.

Diane Britton

I HAD A FATHER YOU A BROTHER WHAT A MAN

He walked where angels feared to tread,
The jokes he played, stories he could tell of times gone by
working down the mine.
He learned the hard way, from the age of eleven,
Yes, he took it in his stride, as he did all his life.
Just a second ago, he asked for a cigarette, *And Died*.

I miss him now he's gone, my father who worked down the mine,
It was though he was hewn out of Welsh rock, but when he smiled
the cragginess melted away, and he was like the laughing waters of
a Welsh stream. Perhaps a little fanciful to suggest, but permissible
when we talk about a Welsh man, as we all have a wild romanticism
deep in our souls.

When you lay a miner to rest in the ground, in a sense he is going
home to his eternal element; where he can hear the familiar noises
that, punctured his life, and indicate that work still goes on.

But his soul, his essential being, has gone to God, so be careful
how you talk of Dad, my father, your brother.
He hasn't gone away, he's gone to where mortality is swallowed up
by immortality.
Where men dwell not in flickering shadows, but in the blazing light
of God's new day.

Freda Biggs

MORE TO LIFE

My whole life was resurrected upon
Lies and deception, until you came along.
You showed me the truth behind all the fiction
You rescued my soul from mass restriction.
You guide me to the light I do desperately seek,
You take my mind higher than the highest mountain peak.
My whole life has changed since you came along,
You brighten my day like a mid summer song.
You warm my heart and like a candle flame glow,
My whole life could end with just one simple blow.
Without you, the ending would all make sense,
Without you the pain would be immense.
You are the only truth behind all the lies,
Behind all aggravation, behind the cries.
Yourself alone can make me see,
There is more to life than just misery.

Helen Lewis

UNTITLED

At 5 o'clock my work is done,
I head for the car park and setting sun,
Through traffic maze, noise and fumes,
I spy the sea through golden dunes.
I'm on the motorway heading east,
The traffic thins, I feel at peace.
I'll have my tea, and do my chores,
Then doze on settee to contented snores.
Life's circle occurs every day,
But to break the pattern without dismay.
To seek another exciting path,
And face adversity with a laugh.

Joe Waterman

THE BENCH

Two people sit on their garden bench, deeply wrapped in thought,
Each touching a lion's head, cold, green, man-made iron wrought.
Their thoughts drift towards days so long gone
When tranquil moments like these, there were none.
Their progress dogged by three sets of feet,
Each would want to squeeze onto this nice shiny seat.
With their memories they cherish together as one
They look at each other, with eyes full of fun.
Together they go back to the day 'their three' found dead
A lifeless bird, 'their three' so lovingly cared.
With her bra as a coffin, the three pall-bearers went
To the grave in the garden, all so solemnly meant.
They travel back to the time when a rabbit he had to kill,
In pain 'poor bunny' no cure, no miracle pill.
Three pairs of moist eyes, turn their backs and start walking
He, the villain, to him, they 'weren't talking'.
Control of their facial muscles they both lose,
As she reminds him of their first Christmas goose.
Prepared so carefully, she cooked the fine bird
On Christmas Eve morning, not a sound could be heard.
Six greasy hands, and not one clean face
No plump goose, an empty carcass in its place.
Nobody touched it, three mouths said,
'Not us mummy,' 'We were in bed.'
They don't hide their joy from each other no more,
To other treasured memories they let their thoughts go.
To them both, this is their little bit of heaven on earth,
Each privately giving thanks to 'their three' given birth.
They have both given their all, made sacrifices along the way,
Just to get this afternoon, one sunny Sunday in May.

Karren Kinsey

CONFUSION

Who's taking all my memories?
Who's meddling with my thoughts?
I strive to keep my dignity,
What is this cruel force?
Each day I wage a battle,
Chasing shadows from my mind.
Then I retreat to childhood,
Seeking something I can't find.
I try to tell my story -
Words stumble on my tongue,
Where is my gown of nonchalance
I wore when I was young?
Now I feel imprisoned
I no longer comprehend.
Is my visitor a stranger, husband,
Daughter, son or friend?
I glimpse the world through windows,
No role for me to play.
Life! Please let me go
No reason now to stay.

G Priest

FALLEN HERO

Nation's leader,
brash, idealistic.
Full of dreams,
full of hope.

Within a moment,
full of madness.
A sniper leaves a world
full of sadness.

Broken dreams,
broken promises.
Tears abound in a world
astounded.

Mortally wounded,
a hero, dead.
Gone is the grace,
gone is the pride.
A hero has fallen,
fallen dead.

Suzanne Swift

I TAKE NO PRISONERS

Whatever I own I usually lose,
To conquer your soul would be self abuse.
To capture your heart I'd need no excuse,
But I don't want a prisoner of war.
I don't want to take till I can't take no more,
All I want is for you to be you, loving me.
All I want is for me loving you tenderly.
You're a woman of courage, daring and pride,
Intelligence and beauty inside.
Do you yearn for embrace that won't hold you down?
Do you weep at night but not make a sound?
If you do don't cry for me yet,
Because I'll treat you with deserving respect.
For me it would be strange to
Change and rearrange you.
No, I don't want a prisoner of war,
You're perfect the way that you are.

David L Brown

GOODBYE GWENT

Goodbye Gwent! I'm leaving you,
There must be better things,
Just waiting out there, for to do
A life that's fit for kings.

I'm going where there's lots of jobs,
And shops to spend my wage in.
A place that's never heard of yobs
Just solitude to bathe in.

I'll buy myself a lovely house
That has no burglar alarm.
No security light or padlocked gate,
A cottage full of charm.

I'll leave my back door open, for
It's safe to do just that.
The people there will smile all day
And stop to have a chat.

The children there will play outside
And skip and laugh all day.
They'll use cardboard to make a slide
And picnic in the hay.

Now where's this place, it can't be far,
I'll study on the map.
Then load my stuff into the car
And get out of this trap.

The world's my oyster, shall it be
Brighton, Devon or Kent.
France, Bangkok or Waikiki
Anywhere is better than Gwent.

I know the place, but can't go there,
I've realised . . . at last.
The place that I've been yearning for
Is somewhere called 'The Past'.

Meryl Anne Parfitt

GWENT

People come from far and wide
To the valleys and the hills
They came here just to hide
From the City and the pride.
And gazed in wonder, in awe,
As they walked and looked around,
Oh the beauty that one saw,
At last, utopia had been found.
Undulating mountains, every mile or so,
Springs that trickle from high above,
They wanted to see more.
They liked and fell in love,
To a life so free from frenzy.
In hamlet, village and in town.
That others would just envy
All these things I had forsook
For granted till they came.
Forest, river, lakes and brook
To me was all the same.
Sheltered from the fierce gales
By mountains all around.
This county of Gwent in Wales
My resting place I've found.
Now I move, with legs I walk
All the sights I see.
Verdant, meadow, rabbit, hawk,
Hedgerow, flowers, trees.

C McCarthy

SHEEP SHEARING 1940 NANTMEL RADNORSHIRE

Come my boys, it's the end of May
And time to fix the shearing day
The sheep must shed their winter coat
Like peerless ermine gracing stoat.

A pound of wool's but eighteen pence
That is our meagre recompense
But risk of maggot is too great
To leave their coats in such long state.

We'll gather first the topmost hill,
And then the valley ground until
Every ewe and lamb is found
Especially in the ferny ground.

The flock was gathered one by one,
And housed near homestead out of sun
And dogs and ponies rested too
Before another day was due.

Meanwhile the farmer's wife made start,
On baking pies and apple tart
And roasted beef with dumplings fat,
Bustled around and shooed the cat.

Next morning came and neighbours too,
Ready to clip the whole day through
The barn was clean, benches supplied,
Around the floor and sheep's legs tied.

The steady snip of shears all day,
Soon made their mark and fleeces lay
Ready to roll and put in sack,
A shearer arched his aching back.

The pitch-pot bubbled on the fire,
Each sheep was marked and loosed from byre
And ere the edge of night had come
The weary shearers made for home.

William Austin Pugh

BEAUTIFUL GWENT

The hours turns into minutes as time ticks past,
The changes of Gwent are happening fast.
Looking around me what do I see?
Fields of rich and so green,
With no trace of coal dust that once had been.

The water in the rivers glitter in the sun,
Children playing in the parks having so much fun.
Daffodils and tulips dance in the breeze,
All of these things are bright and beautiful to see.

But there are bad things here also that still remain,
And no matter how hard we try we just can't change.
Like the factories no sooner built are ready to close,
Leaving the workers to suffer the blows.
Like the shopkeepers afraid to leave their shops at night,
Like the old people hiding behind their locked doors,
Filled with fear and fright.

But no matter where we go we will always face good and bad,
And no matter how far we travel there will always be happy
and sad.
And no matter how far I have to go or how far I have been sent,
I am always glad to return back home,
To that beautiful place named Gwent.

Sian Williams

MY HAPPY WORLD

I can remember happy faces as a child,
Not so many children turned out wild.
For we'd have a smack, get sent to bed,
Full of guilt and nothing said.

Eyes all glistening with a tear,
Still praying Mam is oh so near.
We'd look for forgiveness from our mother,
For in hearts we'd have no other.

For in my world, everyone cared,
Nobody or nothing ever compared.
And we would run, when mother would beck,
That special word we'd call respect.

Yes respect was the word,
Children seen, but never heard.
For my mother to me gave birth,
She put me on that happy earth!

But now the world has turned so very bad,
And makes me feel so really sad.
With drink and drugs, children battered,
In my world everything mattered.

Now people fight and cause much violence,
And yet this world will sit in silence.
Not too often will people come,
That's not until, something bad's been done.

So what's gone wrong, and why do I cry?
No-one knows, and don't ask why.
There's no more work, and no more money,
Not even summer, we now call sunny.

There's no more laughing, no more singing,
No more on Sundays, the church bells ringing.
No more thought, just sheet hate,
Now this is my world, and what a state!

Stephanie Jenkins

REMEMBER

I remember the miners who walked
        Down my street.
Black were their faces and weary
        Their feet.
My father, my uncles, my cousins too.
        Friends and neighbours with scars
            Of blue.
They toiled at the faces to hew out
        The coal.
That fired our ships that took on the
        World.
From sun up to sunset they worked
        Down the mine.
Cap lamp on helmet for them did it shine.
        Through the dust and the darkness
            That they knew so well.
To the testing of the roof that should
        Sound like a bell.
This tells the miner that all is well.
        Most returned home for family
            To greet.
But many a miner's ascent was not
        So sweet.
I remember the miners that never
        Walked back down my street.

T R Llewellyn

THE MIGHTY HEART OF WALES

Dear rich Englishmen,
Sat in your houses of gold,
Have you heard the stories,
That our Welsh hearts have told.

Of our anguish and our sorrow,
Our misery and despair,
The sacrifices we have made,
To fill with gold the lion's lair.

Have your heard the tales of courage,
Of men who face death each day,
And of us helpless wives,
Who can only get down on our knees and pray.

Pray for the lives of men,
They could not save,
And for the children you have lead,
Into their early graves.

For your pride and your riches,
You have raped a land,
Stole the coal from off our hands,
From countries afar,
You have gained your sales,
But you cannot drain,
The mighty blood that runs through Wales.

Leanne Chapman

GOTHIC ROMANCE

The great tragedy of romance
is how it can, like sweet dreams,
turn into a nightmare,
far removed from the idyll that has been;

when those we once trusted and
contentedly idolised,
inspire only horror
as they terrorise and haunt our lives.

Paul Megycks

THE RAINBOW FIELDS

Beneath the dusty swirling clouds
beneath the mischievous sky
lies the rainbow field
a place of many colours and variations
within this field lie the roses
dancing in the wind with their naked beauty
at one with the sky as the moon is at night
An army of life and dreams.

The roses stand so firm
their roots their foundations
living in the wind
the flower so fragile
so easily trampled
alone they will fall, together they thrive
So weak, yet so strong.

As the sun weeps the sky's tears
the flowers worship the sun as their God,
yet some choose to worship the rain,
Or the wind that carries their seeds through the air.

Throughout the rainbow field,
the roses live in harmonious pollination
under the burning sun from which they drink
the fruits of life,
for as long as they have the sun, earth, rain and wind
They need not want for anything else.

David Vaughan Lewis

MY UNSUNG HERO

Unwittingly to war a young man went that day,
with tear filled eyes I watched him on his way.

A last kiss and goodbye, I was left standing alone,
to never return, how could I have known.

In life he was with me in body and soul,
in death his spirit has taken over that role.

He is the sun which glows in the day,
the warmth I feel he sends my way.

He is the moon that shines in the night,
no darkness I see for he gives me light.

He is the wind whispering through the trees,
his presence is with me through the gentle breeze.

He is the ground underneath my feet,
guiding a path which will always be sweet.

He is the star which shines so bright,
I know it is him, it is a wonderful sight.

He is the world revolving around,
encircling me, keeping me safe and sound.

Why did that young man go to war that day,
did he have a choice, did he have any say.

As I look at the inscription upon his grave,
how can I forget him, that person so brave.

Elsie M Boyle

LONELINESS

There is loneliness within my heart
The loneliness that made us part.
The road of no return has passed
But have I really conquered it at last.
My soul has searched to no avail
For someone adjacent to my plane.
So I wander on in emptiness
Searching for one who will care and trust.
Will I ever find this love I need
I am so wild, untamed and free.
Thus I carry on along the road of no return
Always seeking the one I yearn.
Will someone take my hand
And lead me to a promised land.
Away from pain, away from shame
Away forever from those I have loved in vain.

Clare Louise Mcdonald

SWIMMING

We go swimming each Thursday my friends and I
There's Veronica, Jean, Iris and Nora.
The water is warm as we lazily lie
and think all our troubles are over.

I'm first in the water, can't wait you see,
Jean's next with her impression of dolphins diving
Then Iris all smiles, so glad to be free,
Veronica and Nora are late arriving

So if you would follow us down to the pool -
For pleasure or leisure or playing the fool
There's nothing quite like it the hippo would say
So here's to the next time, hip hip hooray!

Anne Goulbourne

ETERNITY IS LIKE TOMORROW

Black, fast moving, ever changing cloud leviathan,
Moving out of the human frame, enabling the
Eye to observe time in motion, not by means
Of a clock, but as a snapshot of eternity.

Our very being is likewise apart of the journey,
Not separate, darkness will bring with it melancholia
Which is due to allegiance with the past, its people,
Its events, its turmoil.

But water vapour, disguised as cloud, has its
Sights set firmly on the next day of tomorrow,
And somewhere beyond, for here a day has
Quietly passed, but a new lunar day has begun,
A new crescent has emerged.

Out of an old stone wall, has fallen a
Mixed collection of white snail shells,
All empty, in that respect, they are familiar
To eternity itself.

An eternity, still yet to be filled with many
More empty shells, that are not yet even
Formed, thereby enabling thought, based on
Observed experience to triumph over present.

Without past, there can be no future, but
What came first, how could one ever be
Without the other.

Paul G Davies

SUMMER '95

Late August, yet tropical sunshine,
bathes our humble valley . . .
with beams, deepest gold:
glorious sunsets, painted lush;
such a summer! Not known for centuries.

Some flowers, and vegetables even,
withered! Beyond recall;
silver-bands play in the park,
people sit in adoration;
the lake, deep blue grass,
in which large carp, rise for fly.

Jolly little boats . . .
go round the island, and yet around;
children's laughter abound and abound:
great the fountain, dribbles weakly,
trying to please.

Berries heavy, in the hedgerow,
                    coloured early,
hazel-nuts full of their shell;
such a summer to remember . . .
summer times, are the ones to remember.

Bleak winters, may come and go,
frozen pipes, chilled fingers;
deep-draped snow, so white,
icicles grow as if by magic in the night:
but, all is forgotten, when summer gold,
                    comes again.

Bernard Williams

LIFE

Life passes you by
And it doesn't tell you why
It's such a funny thing
It starts in the spring
In the summer it's fun
Lots of things to be done
In the autumn you slow down
You have time to look round
In the winter you've found out
But you're unable to shout
And you're too old to care
When you're stuck in a chair
So do what you can
Be you woman or man
Get the most out of life
Don't cause trouble or strife
Do good every day
Make the most of your play
And in the end you'll be glad
You were good and not bad

Joyce E Williams

THE WELSHMAN

Smouldering pride and patriotism
poise confidently
on his strong, square shoulders
as he swaggers calmly through the crowd
of Englishmen.

The red dragon breathes
his unrecognised language,
rusty and barbed,
stumbling from his fiery soul.

His eyes ablaze with honour;
His face set with the dignity
of his people;
The glory of his nation
distinct on his tongue.

No wooden spoon for him.

Vikki Powell

CITY

Fallen fortune, flutter and flicker,
Cast light upon the day,
Take away shadows, darkness dulled,
Clearing mist, morning dew.
Far from a place of emptiness, silence,
The city lays, chaotic and cursed,
The last flower blooms,
Bursts from within the bud
To be trodden to the ground.
Cruel city streets.
Collected at the foot of a wall
The dust of the day
To bring bleakness to all.
A monument of human folly stands,
Raised from fog, swirling smog,
One city tower far above a thousand more.
Glass panes covered in wintry ice,
Intricate patterns on a painter's picture scene.
Moon sparkles on watery ways,
She peers through slanted curtains
Upon the city's blackened blindness
As the last ship leaves the dock
Then silence again falls 'til morning calls.

Cruel city streets.

G Elvira

ALL QUIET NOW

I search for a reason
Nothing comes
Silence

I look in their eyes
They deny
Silence

I look in the mirror
Who is she
Silence

I watch the door
No-one knocks
Silence

I wipe my face
Never dry
Silence

I'm not alone
But so bereft
Silence

I tend her grave
Daisy chain
Silence

I call her name
Constantly
Silence

I search for answers
There are none
Just, silence

Roy Wyatt

THE DRAGON

Here in Wales in days gone by,
the dragon it did live.
It slept by day in cold, damp caves,
and walked around at night.

From the eyes of man,
they used to lay an egg.
This big red vegetarian,
it led such a restful life.

Until they breathed out fire,
to make the night-time light.
They loved to swim in rivers or the open sea.
Sometimes with the fishes,
in perfect harmony.

Now we don't get to see them,
they now live underground.
Everyone thinks they're extinct,
but I have got a photo,
I found it on our flag.

If you ever see one,
do not be afraid.
Take a colour photo,
and have the picture framed.
But, please keep it a secret,
from all other creeds.

There cannot be many left,
so show how much you care.
Pretend that they are fiction,
and they will never end.

Remember every Welshman is a Welshman to the end,
believers in the dragon, a folklore told by men.

Thomas John West

WINTER

Through my kitchen window
I can see
The bare brown branches
Of a mountain tree.
The frost has covered
The roof of my shed,
The hedgehog's gone to sleep
And the flowers are all dead.
The cats are curled up,
They peacefully doze
In front of the fire,
While I warm my toes.
I hate the long, dark nights
And the bitter cold,
Somehow, I seem to feel it more,
Now that I'm growing old,
Still, spring will surely come
And one day I'll see
Little green buds
On the bare mountain tree.

E M Davies

THE GARDEN'S CALL

As winter's mantle starts to lift
Giving way to warmer days
I feel the garden calling me
As upon its beds I gaze.

A plan of action needed here
To put the place in order
To teeze the weeds out from the beds
and the lawn back from the border

The soil is soft and crumbly
and releases weeds with ease
But it isn't long before I feel
The pangs in back and knees.

A stretch and walk is needed now
and survey the work that's done
There'll be more pain for back and knees
Before the battle's won.

Iris Puxty

WINTER SCENE

What a change to look out and see,
As the weather is so cold, and it blows,
Yes the wind do blow, and yes we got snow.
It is so white, and the sky is grey,
So we will have snow again, today.

The little birds will find it so hard,
To get their food, because the ground is hard,
So we bought some seed, and some lard,
Mixed them together made them a seed tart,
So we put it outside, for the birds to have a feed.

It is so nice to see the little birds come down,
To see them enjoying, the food we put on the ground.
It is amazing to see the different birds that go for the food.
Big ones, and little ones, and some in between,
They leave behind them, their tiny footprints in the snow.
And after they are full, then away they will go.
The snow is so pretty, and it shines in the sun,
It can also turn to ice, but it will melt when it is done.

Margaret Coleman

A SPECIAL WISH

If a special wish was granted
To everyone on earth
I wonder what my wish would be
And what would yours be worth

Some would wish for lovely hair
Or a really pretty face
Others would want real mink
And dresses made of lace

But if you had a little child
Who was born both deaf and dumb
You'd only wish that little kid
Would shout 'I love you Mum'

People with no feet or legs
Don't wish for fancy shoes
Or people sat in wheelchairs
Just to walk is what they'd choose

A special wish for someone
With eyes that cannot see,
Would only be to see the lights
Upon a Christmas tree.

Why do we wish for fun and games
And all those worldly pleasures
When a little house that's full of love
Is worth a thousand treasures

But you see we are only human
And we don't realise
The things that really matter
Are right before our eyes

N G England

TOO LATE

Cold, grey winding gear rising like a dinosaur between towering heaps of jet black coal,
Reminder of a time now gone, a way of life now just a memory.
A playful breeze plays round the yards, whisking dust into the autumn air,
Only to sprinkle it like pepper onto lines of once clean washing.

Gone are the days when there was work, though hard and grimy toil,
When fathers, sons and brothers worked side by side in dark, damp seams of coal.
Gone are the days when families stayed together from the cradle to the grave,
Always there for one another, in times of crisis and of joy.

Now slowly creeps the tide of change, to wash the valley clean.
A green, but artificial landscape shrouds the land that once stood black and bare.
Embryonic factories huddle together; cheap, prefabricated, not built to last.
New red brick dwellings spring up to house outsiders who will come to take the jobs.
Too late, the change, to save our town, our sons and daughters all have flown.
Too late, for us, for what is left when youth and heart are gone.
Too late.

J M Dickinson

MEMORIES

Close your eyes and dream awhile,
About those yesteryears.
The trees were tall and handsome then,
Green grass quivered in the wind.
This land of ours was beautiful,
Wild flowers scented the air.

Remember all those birds that sang,
The screeching owls around the barns.
Water voles and river pike,
What about the Sunday hike.
Hedges filled with dew strung webs,
Honeysuckle weaving through.

But now it's called the modern world,
Progress when even jobs are lost.
Time we changed our way of thought,
Just glance and see just what its cost.
Open wider, let's get wise,
Thank God we have the open skies.

Jane Lewis

FALLING IN LOVE

Two minds, two souls,
and two hearts entwine
Affection with passion
then love divine

Two bodies join
with strong embrace
Lips touch,
and pulses race

The world still turning
both unaware
Thoughts pass, eyes meet
with fixed stare

Everything now
has joined as one
Only true love
all hate has gone

Craig A Leach

CARING

They tell us that in the ozone layer there's a hole
Over the north and south pole.
Should we worry? Should we fret?
Will more people get skin cancer? You bet!
We recycle paper, bottles, cans
Will we ever save our lands?
Rhinos, hippos, elephants, pandas, are all becoming a dying breed
Just because of the hunters' greed.
People are crying, dying, all for the want of a bit of food
We must share our resources to do some good.
People are fighting, there are wars
Is this one of nature's laws?
No! This is not what we need
We want another moral creed.
People to care for each other and all wildlife
Wanting a bright new world without any strife.
Old people live longer, babies being born
To face the beginning of a new dawn.
We must worry, we must care
Because the human race and earth are so very rare.

Margaret Jones

SNAKE

You step upon my back
Kick me, bury me by your dust,
Mock me as I laugh at you.
For I am death, I shall kill you all,
You drown in your own blood
As you are my slaves
The fire will engulf your very souls
And your ash is lost.

Valley walls are dark,
Scarlet sky, the big black river,
A cloud covers the sun.
Great hills contain the evil within.
Wailing winds mourn for men,
Silent cries are never heard.
Leave your body and fly above the clouds
To the sun, but never go beyond the hills.

Beyond the hills there is an orchard,
Full of rich fruit, feel its power.
My wall begins to crumble
But we no longer fear death,
I am this killer of man.
A snake has no wings,
I will sink in the mud
But I will not be dead

David Haydn Smith

FIRST BORN

I remember well with great content,
That special day and the event,
That brought with unimagined awe
A new creation to adore.
With soft complexion of peaches and cream,
This tiny life was not a dream,
But true and pure in every sense,
Bringing emotions most intense.

Each passing day brought signs anew,
A look, a smile for all to view,
First tooth, first steps quickly made,
Sure-footed, determined, never afraid,
Exploring eagerly each new turn,
Sure of purpose, quick to learn,
Gathering friends with simple ease,
Happy in play, always ready to please.

All too soon the years pass by.
The defiant stage has come, I sigh,
I hold my breath, I wring my hands
For there before me boldly stands,
A restless teenager in full fight,
Battling with all her might,
Maturing now with radiant fire,
The flame increasing ever higher.

Without choice but ride the storm,
Until at last return to norm,
The past forgotten, put to rest,
Happy to survive the test,
A new beginning on solid ground,
For a future strong and sound.

Pamela Dawes

I WONDER WHY

Oh how I wonder each bright new day
What wonder of nature will cascade my way
To see a flower come into bloom with pretty petals
So proud and groomed
Then to see it die far too soon
To see a spider spin its web
To catch some flies in its sticky threads
Or to see a tree shed its leaves
In the cold of the autumn breeze
To see the birds flying by
Flying south to warmer skies
Then to see the snowflakes falling down
To form a great white blanket upon the ground
Oh mother nature I wonder why you create
Such beauty in the blink of an eye
Then you destroy it all
It seems in vain but perhaps it's so
You can start it all over again.

R Llewellyn

SEEING YOU THROUGH

As you proceed down life's mysterious way,
Facing everything, and passing throu'
another day.
You will realise and know it to be true,
That this special love will help to see
You throu'.

You will have your ups and downs.
And people's indifference make you frown.
But then a bird will sing before your eyes,
And this feeling of love will help you
compromise.

We all have our roles to play,
Like actors, fate directs our way.
But also fate guides our destiny,
And this special love will turn into
reality.

Distance and time all play their part,
And sometimes cause an aching heart.
But they can also be kind,
And a way for us eventually find.
So be happy and content my lovely,
For sure enough we will fulfil
Our destiny.

C Alun Jones

SPRINGTIME

Hurrah, hurrah, let us welcome spring.
A time of rebirth for everything
We gladly say goodbye to the frost and snow
And the cold winds that in winter did blow.
Now look at the trees that have stood stark and bare
You'll see new buds growing everywhere:
Bulbs in the ground are growing too
Soon we'll see flowers peeping through,
Gentle snowdrops, crocuses and daffodils tall
We'll soon be seeing them all;
Primroses, violets and bluebells too
Will colour the hedgerows in every hue.
On the fields and hillsides young lambs are at play,
They're glad that spring has come to stay.
We too can shake off the winter blues,
Enjoy the spring and rebirth too.
Thank you God for springtime.

N D Davies

LIVING MEMORY
(For Chris)

Amongst neat, clustered snowdrops and bunched primroses on hedge bank,
stand silent shadows of yesterday,
where once they hand cut, yellow butter, strong blocked cheeses and fresh,
sweet, hay,
beside the laughing rush of water, skipping through tall, cool, trees,
and the touch of a million ploughings echoing in the leys.
I wonder, were they happy homes filled with love, pleasure, song, delight?
Did they watch the buzzards rising in ease-some, blue-skied flight?
The sash-cord window stands framing, back, when time was careful weighed,
though its roof is gone completely and stone built walls, all but, decayed.
If they ever had a garden it's mingled in nature's gains,
and, since they came once from her, the stones she too reclaims,
clothing all in sparkling ivy and skirting with filigree wisps of fern,
dusting over footsteps' pathways with grasses and lucerne.
A stump stands in remembrance of pail-pulled water gathered there,
and elder forces a hundred tiny fissures in what once was the hayloft stair.
These epitaphs of *gone before* though concealed and quiet,
sing loudly of their ancestry, blending to earth's artistic riot.

M C Lawrence

GOLDEN DAYS

She stood on the deck
As natural as the sun.
Up it comes red and gold
Bringing goodness from the holy one.

Hair blowing to the summer breeze,
The woman loves the dawn.
When dreams are free
Like the land and sea
Such things as these are not worn.

Say a prayer for the coming
For grace is in God's hands;
It went down looking beautiful
And came up with the same free plans.

Enlighten my soul O sun so bright
And I will sing your praise.
Bring me a wife
As warm as your life
And we will shine through your
Golden days.

Nick Purchase

HIRAETH

I left in the early sixties
to live in the land of the free
hoping to seek my fortune
which always evaded me,
and life out there
was full of fun
with movie stars aplenty
a few old rockers came my way
"Do you think I'm really sexy?"
Yes, times were cool and crazy then
till hiraeth called to me
she stayed and played
for ten long years
and took the life in me.
So now it's back to my homeland
the mountains so proudly they say
we've waited for you
for such a long time
but why did you go away?

Sandie Page

REMEMBERING

While sitting in the sand
And looking at the sea,
My thoughts wander in land
Thinking of thee.
Beside me you always were,
We shared all, good and bad.
Your vitality was always there,
Now while I think, I am so glad
We have known each other
For so long a time
Never any bother,
Our love sublime.
AS I wander on my own,
Not liking what I feel,
It is a while you have flown,
I pray and kneel.
And continue living.

Enjoy the freedom of nature
Which is everything.
You belong to the future
Continue living.

Ruth Lewis

A BLIND MAN IN APRIL

April would charm me
Could I see
The blossom on the apple tree
The busy blackbirds flying past
Sticks in their beaks; they never rest
A primrose and a mossy bank
And green ferns in the woodland, dank

Yet I can feel each April shower
Upon my head, and every flower
Smells different; each scent lingers
In my mind, my fingers
Feel each tree's rough bark
And with my ears I hear a lark
And running water; and the breeze
As it blows gently through the trees

April would charm me
Could I see . . .

Peter Varley

UNTITLED

The world was a virgin untouched by man,
Untrod by foot, unstirred by hand.
A place full of promise, unseen by fears.
For man, still unborn, but the world held his seeds.
Seeds of an apple that one day would explode.
On a world unprepared for the horror it sowed.
This world, where even harsh death was no more,
Than life's thirsting at times open door,
Where the only gain was time to endure,
And only an uncertain promise was sure.
But man, the destroyer bent all to its knee.
Cursed vilely at that which sought to be free.
And all that which would not bend to his will,
He slaughtered and raped in a frenzy of kill.
Mountains and seas he fought and he tamed.
With the beast within that's never been named.
He's reached to the moon, now his hands seek a star,
For he longs to be king no matter how far,
And though he gains the universe's throne,
He still hasn't conquered the mind that's his own.

A Webley-Parry

EXTINCTION

They say *extinction is forever*,
But do we really care?
By now I'd say we must,
The earth and all the living things,
Well, they deserve a fair chance too.
They're not the only things *He* created from costless dust.
What makes us tick?
Could it be all the money to be made,
From the forest in Brazil?
Or the dough from the tortoise shell?
Or even the bread from the great elephant tusk?
R E S P E C T - find out what it means to me,
To your fellow man, to every creature,
To everything that lives.
We all depend on each other and, at the end of the day,
We should be grateful,
For what the man upstairs gives.
We're not just here to make money, you know,
Remember, it's him who put us here,
It isn't really our place to decide,
It's Him who should take us back.

Emma Curtis

TO THE FUTURE OF THE PAST

I've just been looking
at photos, of times gone by.
It's funny how they make you
stop, think, then sigh,
of those times gone by.

You don't realise,
when things are great,
until times gone by,
and then it's too *late*.

Back then you don't realise
the fun you were having,
when you're dancing, playing and laughing!

But *why* does time
always have to go by?
Maybe some day in time,
we'll have the answer to *'Why'?*

Karen Ann Grady

LITTLE ONE

Precious baby small and sweet
Wrapped in blankets soft and neat
Quietly sleeping in your cot
Cares and worries you have not

Golden hair on pillow white
Sound asleep throughout the night
I wonder what lies in your head
Tiny thoughts of milk and bed

How quickly night turns into day
And in the sunshine you will play
Growing up without a care
Contented with your teddy bear

Soon your birthday will be here
One big happy birthday year
Not so tiny in your bed
When you lay down your sleepy head

I know not where the time has gone
Months have passed since you were born
But memories I have of you
With golden hair and eyes of blue

Linda Williams

THE VOLUNTEER

The Cap'n said 'You must get in condition,
I want you to enter and I want you to win
You know you can do it hard though it may be
And I will track you - from far out at sea

Although you are now well over the hill
If things get bad I will prescribe the right pill
For the sake of us all, crew, me and the boat
Run your heart out to keep us afloat

Go for it! Forget your age
You are destined to be the 'One Peak's Sage'
Rise at dawn and train all day
Cut out booze, throw your pipe away'

There comes a time for the pressed crew
When, by the Cap'n inspired, there is much they will do
And in old age and health failing
They will run their hearts out - and bugger the sailing

For that breed of crew such leadership is reserved
Each of us receives what, for each, is deserved

R B Douglas

LOVE'S HURT

Julian where has love gone?
The perfect vessel for our content.
We tried hard to please,
it was all well meant.
But each would have our way,
no give and take did we display.
So in this perversity love has gone,
and we are free to try again,
pleasant exercise without the pain.

Margaret Cave

STILL C OF E ... BUT NOW, PLC

The Reverend
Albert,
In his trusty
Lada car,
with rusty
Roof-rack ...
Trundled
Far and wide ...
There was
No hiding
Advertising,
Painted on
the doors ...
The Day Glo
Crucifix,
And messages of
Trade,
Free weddings,
Baptisms,
And visits
To your homes ...
And cut price
Cemetery duties,
Candles, flowers,
And
Gentle music
All supplied
Please call me
On my
Mobile phone ...

Wm Paul McDermott

MOTHER'S JOY

Tiny feet
tiny toes
tiny ears
tiny nose
special boy
brings me joy.
Blue eyes smiling
sad eyes shining
stubby neck
I'm a nervous wreck.
Eat your food,
change my mood.
Love you so,
little Mo.

Gaynor Davies

SHE'S STARTING OFF FOR SCHOOL

I'm taking her to school today
The time has come to go,
She is so small and very bright
And I'm sad to see her go.
For five years now we've been as
one we laughed and joked and
cried. But as I walk her through
the gates I feel much more than
pride. I know she has to read and
write and learn these different
things, how to mix and take her
part and maybe learn to sing,
I'll miss my little girl today
And time will go so slow,
But as a mum the time has come
For me to let her go.

A Horton

SPIRIT AND STONE

Dogma browed frowns
Weigh us all down.
We can't get off the ground.

Dog-eared, well-thumbed pages
Written by all the sages
Down through the ages
Weigh us all down
So much, we're all bound to drown
In a sea
Of complexity.

Our monuments of spirit and stone
Surround us, wherever we go.
The excrement of all that we know,
If only a flower could grow
Through the cracks in our edifices,
Shattered dreams and broken promises
Wouldn't matter at all.
What a truly simple joy it would be
Just to see
A flower grow.

Our monuments of spirit and stone
Cause so much blood and tears to flow,
Enveloped in our flesh and bone.
If only a flower could grow . . .
If only a flower could grow.

R E Sharp

SAD

You're as sad
As a bird that cannot fly
As a willow that cannot cry
As a cat that has to swim
That will not try

As sad
As a rat caught
In a trap
As a tree that has
Lost its sap
As a lost explorer
Without a map

As sad
As a polluted sea
As a broken knee
As a slave who is
Not free
As sad as sad can be.

Charles Wright

THE JAPANESE GARDEN

Miniaturely adequate
Precisely shaped
All shrubbery
In its proper place
Flowering to order.

Bow shaped bridges
Over ponds of lilies
There will be
No disorder.

A shady seat
To sit and ponder
And perhaps
To wonder
Why it feels
So still?

David Madeira-Cole

HOME AT LAST

Oh to Dyfed in the spring,
Your shoots are new just being born,
Growing up towards each dawn.
They open with flowers anew, spreading colour over you.
You change your shape as the year passes away,
New horizons, different colours every day.
Each field different, colour and shape,
Down in the valley up on high,
Wherever we look, you're pleasing to the eye.
The roads roll on, up hill and down dale,
Joining villages they never fail,
To make our journey over you,
Colourful, peaceful, you're a splendid view.
But the view of you I think is the best,
When we cross your border, we're home to rest.
At the end of the day, our journey done,
What more could we ask, than to sit out in the sun,
Peaceful and tranquil, beauty all around,
Dyfed you're now my home, I thank the Lord,
For what I've found.

Jill Munday

HOW COULD I HELP MYSELF?

How could I help myself?
                    Tempted, like Gretel into
the house of delights.
                    Eve, wanted her delicious apple.
So, she bit,
                    and found discontent.
Whoops!
                    What a mistake to make.

Woman, I am a woman,
                    The original sinner.
I am, a temptress,
                    Meaning no harm or sorrow.
How can I liken,
                    Eve to me? I am a happy sinner
Apple,
                    So sweet and tender, knowledge of love.

Poor Adam, the unlucky sod!
                    Eve has run off with
The seductive snake!
                    They are happy, laughing at Adam
While he whispers;
                    'Bastard bitch, bastard bitch, bastard bitch.'
The apple,
                    he has tasted, mouldy in his mouth.

Claire Frost

THE MAN

I was looking at you
And the world was cruel
And the light of the sun
Was blocking my sight

You came from beyond a cloud
With silver lining and a silken shroud
And the light of the sun
Stopped shining in my eyes

The circle of life
Means nothing to me
But the day and night
Is what brings memories

In a world of silent improvisation
We strive for the best we can
Not the noisy hardened place we live in
Just where we hide and cry

The dreams of yours
Are the dreams of mine
But yours are dead
And mine are alive

The cage of the mind
Is what we do not need
But a bus pass
To those not so faraway dreams

S W Coombes

HOLIDAYS!

Holidays, holidays,
What a treat,
Pack your bags,
Wash your feet.
Go to the airport,
Wait in the queue
Two weeks in Ibiza,
Phew!
Get to Ibiza,
Jump in the pool,
Splish, splosh, wish, wash,
Now I'm cool!

Nikki Morgan

REFLECTIONS

We always miss the right time to speak about our love
for the people who give us so much pleasure,

We always miss the right time to give the caress that
conveys so much in a touch,

We always miss the right time to smooth the furrowed
brow or ease an aching limb,

We always miss the right time to hold a nervous hand
through am uncertain day,

We always miss the right time to flash the knowing
smile that shares a secret joy,

We always miss the right time to be there in time
of need without word or deed,

When we were young and lusting after life, it always
is the right time,

When years roll on and life burdens increase, it never
seems the right time,

If this is so, then keep these lines and read them at the
right time.

V A Bater

DRAGON IN THE SKY

Smoke puffs cloud celestial lair,
dragon spits fire into the air.
It wings and forks o'er hill and down,
striking pylon blacks the town.
Inside houses safe and warm
mortals harken to the storm,
some with wondrous rapture peer,
others tremble white with fear,
- close the window, draw the blind,
out of sight is out of mind.
Dragon's beyond mortal control,
hark his anger thunderous roll,
industrial gases rising high
destroying life of earth and sky.
Tears cascade life-giving rain
meanders wide across the plain,
through river beds to reach the sea,
ocean and heaven in harmony.
Wrath and sadness spent, abate,
humanity has sealed its fate,
like dinosaurs to be extinct,
all in the time a dragon blinked.

Avril Williams

EARTH

Placed far away beyond your eyes, o'er rolling hills and dales,
encompassing rich pasture and wooded shrubby vales,
Past vast oceans, mighty rivers, ice-clad mountains flying high,
Lies a mystic curved horizon, where land entwines with sky.
For earth you see . . .is but a sphere . . .a rolling stone in space,
Wrapped up . . .cocooned in mystery . . .much like the universe,
No human knows for certain just how it all began . . .mistake . . .
or huge explosion . . .perhaps some master plan.
Yet . . .out this orb of molten rock the continents appeared,
cooled chunks of shifting granite spreading outward through
the years.
And with its timely passing, that sea of wand'ring rock, enrichened
vacuumed atmosphere with gases dark and hot.
Stirred in that turb'lent cauldron primeval force retained, the
ability to vaporise . . .to drift . . .then fall as rain.
Thus did creation come to pass . . .formed countries out that molten
mass, with rifted valley . . .crevice deep . . .high plateau with wall so
steep . . .barren desert, ocean vast . . .mesa . . .canyon . . .plains of grass . . .
created nations with its spore . . .to populate this wondrous globe.
So reach away beyond your eyes o'er forest glade, and mountain high,
fertiled pastures, wooded vales . . .shrubby hillside, rolling dales,
Seek that horizon . . .deeply veiled . . .then touch this earth . . .this
land of Wales.

Wendall Stone

MY VALLEY

Once, long ago in the mists of time,
was a valley called Cwm Rhondda,
She was fair of face, with beauty and grace,
but her hills they did hide the *Black Wonder*.

The barons they came, with money to gain,
her hills to spoil and plunder,
The steel it went up, the shafts they went down,
the black gold, she is forced to surrender.

The men they strive in her bowels to survive,
boys and girls also toiled for their bread.
When the sirens did sing, women dropped everything
and ran like the wind to the pit head.

Down in the depths of her heart she would keep
the poor souls of the miners who die,
Waiting women above, in the silence they pray
to God, with a sob and a sigh.

Then came the day she had given her all,
her veins ran dry, cracked and sore,
Soon she was sealed, her black scars now healed,
how green is my valley once more.

Kaeleigh McGuire (10)

THE BECKONING

I had a dream that beckoned me
A golden bridge across the sea
I took a step I tried to run
The bridge collapsed
and left me numb
A screaming shriek across the sky
I can, not swim
Am I to die
Then I am plucked out of the sea
Forced to gaze upon reality
But all I see it makes me cry
I can't go on I want to die
I'm sure I heard a voice so strong,
Said trust in me
You can't go wrong,
A big strong man arms of steel,
Said look at me, for I am real
He went away . . .I told him go
Said let me make it on my own
I thought he'd gone
but he had not
He's watching me, because I'm lost
To love a man and know not who
Some would say I can, not choose
And so I'll go on as I am
With vivid images of that man,
Whilst the images I see are real
He looks at me
With eyes of . . . steel

Janice

I LOVE YOU FOREVER AND A DAY

I love you, I love you and I know you love me,
I love you, I love you like a bird in a tree,
I know that you love me, I won't fly away,
I love you, I'll love you forever and a day.

I love you like a rabbit in a field of corn,
I know that I've loved you ever since I was born,
If I know you still love me I won't burrow away,
I love you, I'll love you forever and a day.

I love you like a mole who is under the ground,
drilling through his tunnels without making a sound,
he works in his tunnels so dismal and dark,
If he knows that you love him he could sing like a lark.

I love you like a dog who is faithful and true,
you can tell by his eyes that he only loves you,
If you tell him you love him, then come what may,
he'll love you forever, forever and a day.

I love you, I love you like the bird in the tree,
like the rabbit in the cornfield, I know you love me,
I love you like the mole who sings in the dark,
I love you like the dog who can only just bark.

I love you, I love you and I know you love me,
I love you, I love you forever, together we'll be,
I love you, I love you, forever I'll stay,
I love you forever, forever and a day.

L A Brown

IF I WAS NEVER BORN

I'd never see the sun that shines
throughout my every day
Or see the moon and stars at night
casting out their distant light as if to show the way

I'd never see a child grow up before my very eyes
and never see the birds go flying in the sky

I'd never see my wife on a sunny day in June,
Or put my arms around her waist and say that
I love you

I'd never see a tree blowing in the wind
Or watch its buds appear at the coming of spring.

I'd never see a flower coming into bloom
Or ever see a rocket going to the moon

I'd never see a Christmas Day or a fall of snow
I'd never sit upon a chair and feel the fire's glow

I'd never would have gone for walks
across the mountainside
Or laid myself beside a stream and let the world go by

I'd never stand upon a beach while looking out to see
And feel the sand beneath my feet or waves lap over me.

A G Pengelly

MIDNIGHT IN MISERY

Sitting alone in a darkened room
As the hands of the clock
Tick slowly on towards midnight.
Tomorrow draws near,
It's now so close that tomorrow
Is almost today, and I shudder.
I've been dreading tomorrow,
For, tomorrow, you go away.

I could never hold you back,
Never make you stay,
It's best for you to leave,
By going, you'll better yourself.
There's more for you there, than,
Than there ever could be here,
Than I, or anyone else,
Could ever offer you.

Our last meeting was tense,
A couple of drinks,
Some very stilted conversation,
And that was it.
You had nothing more to
Say to me, nor me you.
You've your own thing to do.
I'm not part of it.
But I'll miss my darling,
While she's away
To me, you'll always be
My little baby girl.
Take care.

James Heaton

ACQUIRED MEMORIES

Times were hard, sometimes sad
We knew both, didn't we Dad
Before Dad died his would be
his sons stay close just for he
Although I tried it's not to be
for now they've both deserted me
Like long lost brothers, so I'm told
while I go out and sit alone
I tell myself that I don't care
But deep inside the hurt is there
Good times we had together Dad
times my brothers can never have
We sang together you and me
they'll never know our harmony
I sit and watch the bar room door
But you won't walk in any more
so sad I felt each week at nine
when tears would roll from my eyes
Two pints I'd order now it's one
Saturdays are no more fun
Christmas Eve is worst to bear
now that Dad's no longer there
we'd sing our carols, ones best known
Until it's time to stroll off home
No more bikes to bring from hiding
Then down the street we'd go riding
sneak them in by the fire
These are memories I've acquired.

Lyn Thomas

REDUNDANCY

When all's despair and hope is gone, as panic calls when day is done
Restless nights and anxious days of worry -
in the endless maze of life

Striving to maintain the norm, filling in the endless form
knowing in your heart of hearts
you simply cannot reach those parts of life

Grit your teeth and on you go, best foot forward to the fore
but deep inside you feel the hurt -
have had your fill of all the dirt of life

Fairweather friends - they play no part to help to mend a breaking heart,
They only want you at a price,
if they can have the bigger slice of life

Oh, dear God, life isn't fair - some get all, and some aware
that they will never ever be
blessed by the eternal tree of life

There's no escape, the pit gets deeper, the road is long the climb is steeper
Collecting dole on pension day
soon becomes the tedious way of life

Must keep on and never show how desolate and very low you feel,
must keep that cheerful smile intact -
beneath which lies the anguished fact of life

Perhaps, one day, your luck will change and life for you will rearrange,
that letter dropping to the floor
might open up a whole new door of life

Christine C Jones

OAK TREE

Have you seen an oak tree,
blowing in the wind.
Felt the bark so thick and rough,
such a wondrous thing.

Leaves so green for all to see,
its branches oh so strong.
The oak tree and the acorns,
go on and on and on.

When the rain is falling down,
you can shelter there.
But if thunder it should start,
you must be aware.

If these oaks could only talk,
the stories they could tell.
Of days gone by and long ago,
they outlive old, old men.

They stand so big and tall,
live through war and peace.
Can't get involved with politics,
what a restful life this is.

It's seen so much life and death,
heartbreak and romance.
Seen the fool and clever man,
and only has one chance.

The birds that rest,
and build their nests
in this tree so strong.
Respect this is, not like man.

S M West

WHERE HERONS WADE

Where herons wade by waterfall,
Kestrels hover, curlews call,
Squirrels dart and act the fool,
Reds are long gone, greys now rule.

Tawny owls in silent flight,
Hunting voles is their delight,
Cross our path, yes once or twice,
Hoping we'll disturb field mice.

Now Welsh mountain ewes give birth,
When they do they show less girth,
Lambs will suckle then lie still,
While sharp-eyed mother eats her fill.

Whilst mother is busy, lambs have fun,
They dance and frolic, leap and run,
Muscle grows strong, as does leg bone,
Soon they're ready for life on their own.

Now curlew chicks emerge from cover,
To answer calls of anxious mother.
Soon they'll fly, then make their way,
To winter near coast, I'd say.

Heron chicks will take to the air,
To cover their district; fish beware!
Parents show them a favourite pool,
Teach them to fish, what a super school!

Where herons wade by waterfall,
Tiny elvers answer nature's call.
They've journeyed far, from Sargasso sea.
Not to grace chef's menu at the heronry!

Charles Ivor Morris

ANIMAL LOVERS

The headlines screamed of cruelty:
A dog thrown from a crag!
But no one mourned the crocodile
Who died to make a bag.

The cat found drowned inside a sack
Was instant front page news.
But no one cared about the sow
Whose hide made pig skin shoes.

A seal was clubbed and people cried,
How can men do such things?
Then calmly ate their chicken roasts
And threw away the wings.

A group was formed to save the whale,
The media praised their zeal.
But no one fought to save the lambs
Who died to make a meal.

We pollute our streams and rivers,
So plants and fishes die.
Our factories belch out poisons,
Which kill the things that fly.

Plant life, insects, birds and beasts
Man decimates it all.
His disregard for all that lives
Will one day be his fall.

B G Waller

WEDNESDAY

On Wednesday I climbed a mountain
And the air I breathed was free.
It made me lose my troubles
With the beauty I could see.

The ocean raised its mighty waves
That curled and crashed in white.
The things I saw, I must confess,
Were a pleasure to my sight.

And then the sun sank slowly
And it left a trail of red.
The blues, the greys, the oranges,
The colours filled my head.

I walked back down the mountain
And saw the city lights,
The cans, the cars, the smoky streets
The buildings with their heights.

So as I walked the city streets,
I thought what man's achieved
And compared to nature's garden,
I suppose that man is but a seed.

I Waller

FRIENDSHIP

Friendship is something that cannot be bought
Friendship is something that has to be sought
For a friend is someone who's there to care
And at your side they'll always be there.

A friend will listen to your joys and pain
And a friend will help you through your life to gain
Happiness or sadness whatever it's to be
If it's sadness they'll set it free.

A friend will be there to wipe away your tears
And help you battle through your fears.
Your innermost secrets you can tell to your friend
Knowing they're there with a hand to lend

They make you smile when inside you're sad
They cheer you up and make you feel glad.
Glad to know you have a friend so sweet
Glad to know you both did meet

For friendship so good should last a long time
And I'm so glad you're a friend of mine
And a best friend at that - I must thank you
For such good friends there are so few

Like sisters we know where we're both coming from
And I think it will last very long
We have a laugh and we have some fun
We always get out as often as we can

So much in common - nothing's too great
You'll get through anything with a best mate
So here's a 'thank you' the best I know how
'Good everything' to you - always and now.

Tina Taylor

THE LONELY PEOPLE

So many people when old age comes along
Every little thing seems to go wrong.
They think of the full life they have led
And it seems to them they're already dead.
The children that they bore
Don't seem to care anymore.
They are all wrapped up in a life of their own
And they forget the ones that are now alone.
They have their house or maybe it's a flat
But home's a place with loved ones on the hearth mat.

The young don't mean to be unkind
Maybe they have other things on their mind.
So many things they have to do
No time to think of the lonely who
Brought them up to what they are
Without the old folk they would not have gone far.

So if only the daughters and also the sons
Would spend a little time with the old ones.
Then maybe their old age will be
Just a little bit less lonely.

Just think of the time ahead
One day it may seem that you're already dead.
When your family have grown and you are parted
I hope they will not leave you broken-hearted.

Tina Simpson

SHADOWS OF THE FIRE

Dancing wildly around the room,
Where the shadows from the fire,
The wind howled outside the door,
But she sat there trying to recapture,
Her memories of the past.

She looked across the room
to the sideboard,
Where on it stood his picture,
She remembered the times when
they sat there together,
She remembered the times they
had quarrelled.

But she wished he could be there now,
To hold her,
Especially in her time of pain,
Inside her she knew her
time had come.

Soon she hoped she would
be with him,
In that wonderful place
called paradise.

Now the room grew darker,
The dancing flames settled
down,
They looked almost lifeless
to her,
Maybe now that woman
knows for herself,
That everything lives after
death.

Sas

THE CRYSTAL

A molten orb hurtles through space,
Orbiting its star at a regulate pace.
As mother earth cooled I took my form,
A crystal born of the fire's storm.
The aeons sped by and I saw it all,
Ice fields vast, volcanoes tall.
I saw the dinosaur come and go.
Fierce lava streams, soft rivers flow.
Before I could settle on my bed eternal
Along came man with his tools infernal.
Gouged and hacked me from surrounding strata.
Cut and polished me, used me for barter.
Adorning the mighty and the fair,
Wrought to shape with craft and care.
Invention arose from man's mental fog,
The age of electronics had all agog.
But the age of crystal wasn't to last,
With technical knowledge man advanced so fast.
So I, once riven from living rock,
Now measure time within this clock.
But from this duty I will never swerve.
Ordained by God, mankind to serve.

J D A Tickle

FIRES IN THE CLOSE

Fires burn in the close.
One moment night -
let grey slide in
and circumvent these trees.

The lamps of the earth
spangle the trodden leaves
that lie like death,
an ashen golden mound
with copper hearts.

Fires in the close,
lamps in the night.
Softly runs the day
to dusk and still.

Away the thoughts
of man of thought
for I am here, and of this glow,
and in the trees, and of the trees
a crackle-buzz of life:
as day eats day and us.

For we are this blank,
this charm, this calm,
nature's nothing
that occupies the day.

Paul Kearns

WINTER'S EDGE SNOWCRUST AT OWL DUSK

Dusk is freezing on moors below.
Slowing down time in cloud reel.
Sliding close! To trees a raw polished claw.
That no longer can feel for frostbite, tho'
The toad blue at night like a planet in its
Heaven can oscillate beneath a gatepost
or pulsate a momentary vehicle . . .
Few alone come to this place
Darkly the owl sighs, for in its feathers
Shadowy seldom moves like lace.

Snow crusting by the baggy wood.
The clock strikes a rationed hour, day encapsuled gale
Sings like a vice, winter onset screws swift allay, in
Blue-pitch night, as the mouse, the vole lay
curled, notched down with holed-up sleep.
Within their snore-hollow, rooting deep.
The snail dry in the chinks of bole.
The owl at midnight hunts - echo hooting bowers.
Crenellated geometry, deep root tubers
Steep miniatures to clear towers.

Dawn slides twilight to drab edge, snow starred sky.
Sparrows scutter lost in ivy block gutter.
Their warm hollow eyes shut close in draught.
The ox bellow falls on cumber iron-hoovéd trough. Solid
-hard moor a star falls thro' icebar floor. At moon
'Tu whuu' bare - let ridge owl seeks church barred yew!
To shed light pellets, silvery shredding thro!
While wind-pangs sail, Barnedge - her call low too!
Snoring platform fast-in-frost, mice turn taloned
'Tu-whit-too-wuu!'

Neville Carlton

MY FRIEND FROM THE SKY

What was that noise? Was it footsteps?
Oh please don't come tonight.
I dare not breathe, I dare not move,
My body is rigid with fright.
Where are you my friend? Please come to my aid,
You know that I'll be hurt tonight.
I need you right now, don't leave me alone,
Hold my hand, help me put up a fight.
Alcohol, I can smell alcohol, I know that he's on his way,
Drunken sounds of clumsiness fill me with dismay.
I can't get out of this room,
I can't scream, I can't shout.
A wave of nausea fills my mind,
There is no easy way out.
I see his shadow approaching me,
And I know that it's me versus him.
Just as I think that my heart will explode,
Everything goes dim.
My friend has come, he has lifted me out,
I am wandering through the air.
The body on the bed is being tortured,
He doesn't realise that the girl is not there.
he doesn't know that the mind is stronger than the body,
And that he's only hurting the physical form.
He doesn't care he's getting what he wants.
He does not care that the body's not warm.
I travel the air aimlessly,
Until he's gone and so has the pain.
I say goodnight to my friend from the sky,
But know that tomorrow night I'll see him again.

Helen Newman

TO A TREE

Silent sentinel of lovers' tryst
Rarely noticed, seldom missed.
Nature's child
By the sky god kissed,
We love you.

Tiny acorns to mighty oaks
From my eye a teardrop coax
In sorrow
At mankind's cruellest hoax.
We need you.

Gnarled but knowing protector of life
In a world full of envy, danger and strife
Beauty unsullied
Where hatred is rife
We use you

The scythe of our avarice leaves branches bare,
A trunk without children, no-one to care
Or remember
What glory was there.
We spurn you.

But you hold the final card
If gone for ever, we're ozone charred.
Guilty fear
O'erwhelms us - be on your guard
We beg you.

Joanne Lavender

DIANA

A tale of woe
of broken dreams
the one you trusted,
is not what he seems.
A dashing knight,
in armour bold,
deceit begins,
the tales unfold.
St George did slay
the Dragon fierce,
its scaly skin,
his sword did pierce.
A legend there
was born of him,
who chanced his soul,
his life and limb.
Alas! Dear lady,
your trust was wrong,
this knight betrayed
your maiden song.
'Tis true he heard
your fearful cry,
but help and guard,
he did deny.
What legend will
abound from this
the man who stole
a lady's kiss,
who fed the serpent
more or less,
and slew the damsel
in distress.

David Price Edwards

SYMPHONY OF VOICES (CURSE OF SCHIZOPHRENIA)

Voices crouching, hidden by your darkness within.
Your eyes betray a subtle, unspoken lament,
Tears writhe in streams of torment.
Although the writing's on the wall,
Did you read the words at all? Did you see us?
Through the echoes of your dream,
We can hear your primal scream, do you hear us?
Reflected in the shards, fragments of shattered sanity,
The cracked mirror of your soul.
Do you know us? Do you know?
Inside your head, we itch with our intrusion,
Escort you to Hell, feed on your delusion.
Our presence will possess you,
Lewd suggestion, depress you; we are:-
The Symphony of Voices,
Come along, sing our song,
We see the tune does not impress you.
We will crawl the walls of your mind,
Like remnants of a nightmare, how wretched.
Shake your head, try to scatter us,
We grip tight, your thoughts are our anchor.
Here we sit, Judgement Day, a subliminal jury,
To slaver on your despair, and spit on your fury.
Listen to our whispers, mock you, taunt you,
Look at our images, brutal visions to haunt you.
You're in here amongst us, downtrodden from view,
Do you still know, which one of us is you?

Sue Butcher

INFORMATION

We hope you have enjoyed reading this book - and that you will continue to enjoy it in the coming years.

If you like reading and writing poetry drop us a line, or give us a call, and we'll send you a free information pack.

Write to

>Anchor Books Information
>1-2 Wainman Road
>Woodston
>Peterborough
>PE2 7BU